# RETHINKING RACE

INDIGORIVER
PUBLISHING

# RETHINKING RACE

### Deconstructing the Categories
### Behind Power and Prejudice

DR. KEVIN COGHLAN

MAUREEN PELEGRIN

*Rethinking Race: Deconstructing the Categories Behind Power and Prejudice*

Library of Congress Control Number: 2025918373
ISBN: 978-1-964686-75-2 (paperback)   978-1-964686-76-9  (ebook)

Although this publication is designed to provide accurate information about the subject matter, the publisher and the author assume no responsibility for any errors, inaccuracies, omissions, or inconsistencies herein. This publication is intended as a resource, however, it is not intended as a replacement for direct and personalized professional services.

Editors: Abigail Dengler
Cover and Interior Design: Emma Elzinga

Printed in the United States of America

First Edition

3 West Garden Street, Ste. 718
Pensacola, FL 32502
www.indigoriverpublishing.com

Ordering Information:

Quantity sales: Special discounts are available on quantity purchases by corporations, associations, and others. For details, contact the publisher at the address above.

Orders by US trade bookstores and wholesalers: Please contact the publisher at the address above.

With Indigo River Publishing, you can always expect great books, strong voices, and meaningful messages. Most importantly, you'll always find . . . *words worth reading.*

*For my best friend, Ronnie*

# Contents

INTRODUCTION . . . . . . . . . . . . . . . . . . . . . . . . . . . . . . . . . . . . .IX

1 THE DAY I REALIZED I WASN'T "WHITE" . . . . . . . . . . . . . . .1

Challenging Our Narratives . . . . . . . . . . . . . . . . . . . . . . . . . . . .8

2 THE INCONSISTENCY OF RACIAL CATEGORIES. . . . . . . . .11

Race As a Social Construct . . . . . . . . . . . . . . . . . . . . . . . . . . . .15

Racial Categories in America . . . . . . . . . . . . . . . . . . . . . . . .17

Racial Categories Around the World . . . . . . . . . . . . . . . . .23

3 THE ORIGINS OF THE RACE MYTH . . . . . . . . . . . . . . . . . . .25

The Language of Division in America . . . . . . . . . . . . . . . . . .28

The Creation of an "Elite" Class . . . . . . . . . . . . . . . . . . . . . . .32

Racism As a Societal Pillar . . . . . . . . . . . . . . . . . . . . . . . . . . .34

4 WHAT SCIENCE SAYS ABOUT RACE. . . . . . . . . . . . . . . . . . .37

**Myth 1:** Race is based on geography. . . . . . . . . . . . . . . . . . . .38

**Truth 1:** Race is *not* based on geography. . . . . . . . . . . . . . . .39

**Myth 2:** Race is divided by physical features. . . . . . . . . . . . .42

**Truth 2:** Similar appearances do *not* reflect similar DNA. . . .43

**Myth 3:** Race is divided by common DNA. . . . . . . . . . . . . .44

**Truth 3:** Racial categories do *not* accurately group people according to common DNA. . . . . . . . . . . . . . . . . . . . . . . . . .45

**Myth 4:** One race can be genetically inferior or superior to another. . . . . . . . . . . . . . . . . . . . . . . . . . . . . . . . . . . . . . . . .48

**Truth 4:** No racial group can claim genetic superiority. . . . .49

5 How Race Upholds Power Dynamics . . . . . . . . . . . . . .53

The Racial Hierarchy Lives On . . . . . . . . . . . . . . . . . . . . . . . .54

How Race Upholds Inequality in Housing . . . . . . . . . . . . .55

How Race Upholds Inequality in Schooling . . . . . . . . . . . .58

How Race Upholds Inequality in Work and Income . . . . .62

The Progress and Setbacks. . . . . . . . . . . . . . . . . . . . . . . . . . .68

6 Reimagining Identity Without Race. . . . . . . . . . . . . .71

The Differences Between Race and Ethnicity . . . . . . . . . . . .73

How Race and Ethnicity Became Adjoined . . . . . . . . . . . . .76

How Culture, Not Biology, Shapes Identity. . . . . . . . . . . . .78

Imagining Culture-Based Identity . . . . . . . . . . . . . . . . . . . . .79

7 Building a World Beyond Racial Categories . . . . .83

Individual Reformation: Confronting Internalized Racism . .84

Interpersonal Reformation: Confronting Relational Racism .87

Institutional Reformation: Confronting Racist Laws, Policies, and Attitudes . . . . . . . . . . . . . . . . . . . . . . . . . . . . . . . . . . . . . .88

Future-Oriented Reformation: Teaching the Next Generation .91

Moving Forward Together. . . . . . . . . . . . . . . . . . . . . . . . . . . .93

Conclusion: The Beginnings of a World Without Race. . . . . . . . . . . . . . . . . . . . . . . . . . . . . . . . . . . . . .95

Acknowledgments . . . . . . . . . . . . . . . . . . . . . . . . . . . . . . . . . .97

Bibliography . . . . . . . . . . . . . . . . . . . . . . . . . . . . . . . . . . . . . . .99

About the Authors . . . . . . . . . . . . . . . . . . . . . . . . . . . . . . . .107

# Introduction

An introduction typically explains why the author wanted to write their book, but I must confess: I did not want to. I have never considered myself much of a writer, and especially after finishing my dissertation, I did not want to sit down and write again. Writing this book was one of the hardest things I have ever done.

However, sometimes a message is just too important. It burns in your mind and demands to be written, no matter how tired you may be. That is how I feel about this message.

The ideas in this book are so powerful that they changed me. But more importantly, I wrote this book because the state of racial relations in the US continues to falter under the weight of prejudice and ignorance.

Racism is a belief that one race is superior to another. It is shocking that people still actually think they are better than someone else based on their race. We are all humans, yet we remain divided.

Growing up, I thought racism was receding to the point that it would die in my generation. Now, I see that I was naive. As I look at society today, covert and overt racism are seemingly everywhere. Whether we see it with our own eyes, on social media, or live on the news, it is impossible not to see racism. After all, if a presidential candidate can be openly racist and still get elected, what does that say about the state of racial relations in the US? It says that Americans not only still tolerate racism but also that many are in favor of maintaining our society's race-based status quo. This has historically been the American way and will be until we begin to change our thinking fundamentally.

What could I do about this? How could I contribute to meaningful change? As these questions kept me up, my mind flashed to my current class of students. I am a psychology and sociology professor who teaches about race and ethnicity, among many other subjects, for a living. I watch my students grapple daily with the push and pull—the progress and the regression—of our society's ability to value and empower all people equitably.

We were reading the textbook for an introduction to sociology class and discussing the origins of race. One of my students said, "Wow. I feel like everything I"ve ever been taught about race was a lie. This should be common knowledge. I think if it were, things in our world would be very different."

I couldn't agree more. Most of what we are taught about race, even into adulthood, *is* a lie, and I believe this is a message that could change not just the way we think of race and power *individually* but also how we conceptualize it as a society.

Of course, advocacy and social change are essential for ending racism, but those efforts alone have not fully succeeded, or racism would not exist today. We've also tried to change the meanings we attach to race, extracting stereotypes and

highlighting the positive associations with various racial groups. Again, while this moves us in the right direction, it has still not fully succeeded in ending racism itself.

I believe that to work toward ending racism, we need something more profound—a fundamental re-interpretation of race in the way my student described it. As a foundation for advocacy and social change, we need an updated ideological basis from which to end racism.

My knowledge about race and ethnicity is continually expanding. Still, this book is an attempt—made by myself and my co-author Maureen, a seasoned educator—to teach what we know about race and ethnicity as we would in a classroom. It aims to help deconstruct the myths you and others have been told about how humanity is categorized and change the attitudes that harm our society.

I am not the first to point out the racial fallacies we have built our society on, but much of the existing writing on the subject is dense and academic—and appropriately so. It is an enormous topic that requires us to sift through history and closely separate fiction and fact from our written records. Yet I know not everyone will pick up a four-hundred-page book on the history of race. Not everyone has the time, even those deeply moved to understanding and action.

Here, I wanted to take a distilled approach to this topic, walking readers through the most salient moments in the creation of the race myth, how it persists today, and what we can do about it.

I see this as a must-read for everyone. If the population adopts the ideas about race in this book, it will positively affect how humans perceive, categorize, and interact with each other on a macro scale. That said, I know this is not a book everyone wants to read. It is hard to confront the idea that everything we were ever told about the biology of race is false.

With that in mind, this book is for those unsettled by what they see around them and want to gain a deeper understanding to contribute to the fight against racist ideologies. If you are here, maybe it is because you are a student wondering about the oppressive and genocidal history of racism. You may be a scholar seeking to understand better the social construction of race and how race structures society. Perhaps you are a person who has always wondered why racism exists. Maybe you know nothing about race but have become curious about the truth behind the veil.

Maybe you are a person who is willing to open your mind to the possibility that race is just a myth. Or perhaps you are just exhausted with the continued subjugation and violence directed towards racial minorities in the US. Whether it's toward you or the people around you, you feel the stress of injustice, and you want a way to fix the social problem of racism.

For me, it doesn't matter who you are—this book is for you because it is relevant to every single person's life. Race is associated with socioeconomic status, social mobility, cultural expression, who we marry, our friends, our internal and social identities, and so on. It affects us all.

I am not naive enough to think this book alone—or any one effort—can end the forces of prejudice and all the other -isms in our society. There will always be people who wish to subjugate others and have no interest in disrupting the status quo. That said, I do believe this book contains the ideological basis for ending racism that should be common knowledge and taught across every educational and cultural institution.

I also understand that the concepts in this book, while not

new, may not be entirely accepted by this generation. Even proven truths take time to seep into a society's common knowledge and functioning.

With an updated worldview, we can tug at the ebb and flow of progress and unravel the race myth as we know it. I hope we can do so together through the paradigms presented in this book.

# CHAPTER 1

# The Day I Realized I Wasn't "White"

To unravel the race myth, I will first tell you how it unraveled in my life. Starting here also allows me to be up-front and acknowledge the fact that I am a pale-faced, red-hued man writing a book about racism. Of course, I have not been the recipient of racism the way many have, purely based on the privilege of my appearance. A person can never completely extract oneself from their experiences to be impartial. So, I don't claim to do that here. In the same way, I will never fully understand the experiences of those who have experienced racial prejudice based on snap judgments about their appearance. So I don't claim that either.

That said, I believe the root of racial prejudice and pain in our society—and the reason I must qualify my position in it—is based on a very flawed and illogical system. I believe that system has cost us the loss of lives, the loss of our humanity, and the loss of lives people could have had access to if it weren't for the "box" of a racial category into which they were born.

My first inklings that our racial categories were not what they seemed to be came from the inconsistencies I found in my own story. This is how that played out for me. I first learned what race I "belonged" to in elementary school. I was about eight years old. I came across the word "Caucasian" on a standardized test that all students had to take in the state of Illinois. When I asked my teacher which circle to bubble in, she pointed at that one. I had no idea what the word Caucasian meant. I remember staring down at the form I was supposed to bubble and thinking, "I'm one of *those*?"

To further complicate matters, the word "White" floated around in the ether. I don't remember how I realized I belonged to that one, too. I assume someone just told me, or I figured it out through osmosis, but I remember beginning to ask the big questions—the questions that stuck with me from my youth to the present. What does it mean to be both Caucasian and White? What does Caucasian mean? It seemed to be a difficult question for adults to answer.

Although I learned I belonged to a race in my youth, I never had a clear sense of what my race was supposed to mean. This could have stemmed from the privilege of being White and never having to consider my race until I had to check a box. It could have also resulted from the lack of diversity in my town. There were indeed many causes.

I only became more aware of my race when my race was compared to somebody else's. I grew up in an upper-middle-class, primarily White town, Crystal Lake, Illinois. The only minorities were well-off Indian families, who, for the most part, were either headed by doctors or engineers.

Never had I seen a Black person in my town until Deron's family moved in. (Obviously, I was too young to understand the systemic roots of why no Black families lived in my town.) Deron was fantastic. Slightly older than me, he had tons of charisma, was super funny, and was a genuinely caring person. He was tall, with bright eyes and dark brown skin.

Deron's family moved to Crystal Lake to place their kids in a good suburb with good schools. My sister immediately became best friends with him, but Deron's family did not stay long, and my sister was soon sad at the loss of her best friend. Deron's family stayed for maybe two years.

Around this time, I started to notice the difference in what it meant to be Black, Hispanic, or Indian, for example, and that being either of those meant being different from White. I still didn't understand the basis for those differences, but I understood they existed. As a kid, I knew enough to realize that being the odd one out in any fashion wasn't necessarily good. I remember wondering, "Did Deron's family leave because they were the only Black family in town, and they felt out of place?" The question went unanswered.

By the time I finished elementary school, I had absorbed much about racial differences and what they supposedly meant. For example, I remember developing one of my first biases in elementary school during the spelling bee. Every year, I would always come in second because I would get destroyed by two daughters of Indian doctors. Rakhee and Kamala, to this day, are some of the most kind and accomplished people I know— they are indeed the best of humanity. They deserved to win, but I still grappled with such a pattern. I remember developing the belief that I'd always get crushed by someone from India because their parents are doctors and they are smarter than I'll ever be. The model minority stereotype had already sunk into my schematic knowledge.

Of course, there was no basis for this belief. Sure, children of immigrants commonly experience the pressure to perform and succeed, fulfilling the dreams that brought their parents to America. But the idea that there was something innate about Indian children that predestined them to beat me at spelling bees was, of course, ludicrous.

When I first told my wife about this childhood belief, she laughed at me. She recounted how when she first came to America as an Albanian immigrant, she crushed the competition in her spelling bee, even though she could hardly speak English. I laughed at myself, too, but it also disheartened me. As a child, I handicapped myself, albeit unconsciously. Blaming it on race made me feel better about losing, as if the outcome was inevitable. But it wasn't. Rakhee and Kamala didn't win because they were Indian; they won because they worked hard. Blaming the outcome on race reduced both of us.

When I got to college, race was not the focus of my life or studies. My obsession has always been with psychology. My doctorate is in psychology. I always say I ended up branching into sociology by accident. That "accident" occurred while finishing my bachelor's degree with minors in history and sociology. I had taken enough sociology classes to double major if I took just one more, so I went back to school for one more class.

In that semester of my bachelor's program, my mind was opened.

I was finishing my sociology degree with a Latin American history class. In that class, I read a book called *Guns, Germs, and Steel* by Jared Diamond. In this book, I came across the word "mestizo." I didn't know what the word meant. So, I looked it up and discovered that mestizo meant Native American mixed with European. My mind grabbed onto this word and couldn't let it go—I sat at the on-campus library late into the night, working through more and more books on the subject.

As I learned more about race and the word mestizo, I pondered my childhood memories. My family was lucky enough to have four generations in one room together. I remember sitting in front of a fireplace listening to the stories of my mom, Barbara, Grandma Gloria, and Great Grandma Nan.

The collective memory of these three generations of women was extraordinary and vivid. My favorite stories were those about my maternal great-great-grandmother, Granny Mag. My great-grandmother, Nan, would tell firsthand stories of her mother, a Cherokee medicine woman. Granny Mag passed away before I was born, but the way Nan described her mother made it feel like she was in the room with us.

Through Nan's stories, I learned how Granny Mag rode bareback on her horse, paced the kitchen with her book of traditional medicinal knowledge in hand, and went out on calls at all hours of the day and night to help people across the hills of West Virginia. As a boy, I always imagined myself riding on the back of her horse, helping her on her essential missions like a superhero's sidekick.

Of course, I am generationally removed from Granny Mag. My suburban childhood was a far cry from bareback horses and medicine books. But still, my family has always been incredibly proud of our Cherokee heritage. Granny was and is still part of me—in my blood, how I viewed who I was and my family's legacy, and how I viewed the natural world around me. Her heritage was part of me, even as America's treatment of indigenous populations has since decimated that heritage.

With these memories circulating, I again visualized the textbook's words. Mestizo means Native American blended with

European. My ancestry is Irish, Welsh, German, and Cherokee. What race did that make me? In Spanish, the word "mestizo" literally means "mixed." Did that make me mixed? Biracial? Was I still Caucasian and White? What mattered most when it came to choosing my racial category? My skin color? My heritage? Where I lived? How others saw and treated me? And what difference did (or should) it make in my life if I now belonged to a different category than I had always been told?

I felt like a child again, sitting dumbfounded in front of a list of checkboxes and trying to understand my place in this convoluted web of definitions and categories—trying to understand who I was and what group or groups I belonged to.

After learning about the word mestizo, I began to question everything I was ever told about race. Why did this shake me the way it did? It's hard to say. Nothing in my life practically changed. Learning this word didn't make me more or less White, nor did it make me more or less Native American. But imagine learning in adulthood that the racial term you had identified with for decades may not be accurate. It was a jarring experience that sent me down a whole new rabbit hole.

Throughout my master's degree, I continued studying race and its origins. I spent the next several years writing as many papers on race as possible. Seeking out knowledge about race became a fascinating compulsion, but it was heartbreaking at the same time. When you study race, you see the violent history. The images of Black people hanging from trees as Whites smile for the cameras, the mutilated and castrated body of Emmett Till, and the bombed-out car containing the remains of Wharlest Jackson still haunt me.

I searched for biological and genetic evidence for the categories I'd been told all my life were social facts. Through my studies,

I finally started finding answers to the big questions. But they were not the answers I expected.

I expected to find a clearer understanding of why different races were biologically different. But as I searched and searched, I saw the truth: there *was no evidence* to support the idea that people of other races are different. Modern peer-reviewed studies explain that genetic or biological differences between various races do not exist. In fact, the use of racial categories only started roughly a few hundred years ago. This was all very strange. We just invented these arbitrary categories out of thin air.

Why would people create these categories? As I probed the question further, the answer was clear. I dove down the rabbit hole of what sociologists call social stratification. **Social stratification** refers to dividing a population into groups that can be ranked hierarchically, meaning one group is placed above another, and their elevated role is then secured through laws and social attitudes. In other words, racial categories were created so that some people could be higher and others could be lower. You can guess which group had the idea for categories like these.

This idea—that racial categories are human constructions and have no basis in peer-reviewed science—transformed how I thought about myself and others. I stopped believing that people of other races and ethnicities were biologically different from me. I had the sense that I could tear walls down that were held in place by the false idea that I was different from someone else. In other words, I found that I no longer wished to identify with a category that was unfounded in biology and existed solely as a mechanism by which to exclude and subjugate others.

# Challenging Our Narratives

Growing up, we are inundated with different belief systems. We are socialized into ideologies that structure our thoughts and behaviors concerning gender roles, religion, political views, social norms, and which team to cheer for. The narratives we are exposed to are very much indoctrinating. We are told they are true and called countercultural if we question authority and knowledge.

Growing up, we adopt many of these beliefs without questioning them. We use them as a foundation for the judgments we make. Sometimes, these judgments that are harmless, like if someone believes their favorite football team is better than another team. However, some of these judgments can be quite harmful to us and others, such as the belief that one race is superior to another. What do we do then?

As a professor, I often joke with my classes about how I must resocialize myself, meaning that I must change my thinking and adapt to new knowledge. This can take simple forms, such as updating my understanding of new slang, like the word "rizz," I picked up from students recently. Resocialization can also involve deconstructing old knowledge as you learn new knowledge.

For example, when I started teaching the sociology and psychology of gender, there was much I didn't know (which is still true now). To name one example, I learned that one to two out of every one hundred people are born intersex, meaning they are not biologically male or female.[1] Not only that, but we have identified *over one hundred* different combinations of intersex. Since

---

[1]    This is directly counter to politicians passing laws stating there are only two genders, when nearly every doctor would acknowledge humans come in at least three sexes.

there are over a hundred combinations of physical traits that can influence gender identity, I am constantly learning about the complexity of how biological processes influence gender identity and how many potential gender categories there are. I must continually update my old knowledge.

There are many perspectives on the topic, but one thing was for sure: the narrative I initially held about gender was not sufficient to describe both the reality and the science on the topic. I needed to let myself be resocialized to understand it in a new way.

When I say things like this to my students, I am modeling what I want them to do: being willing to question everything they have been told. This may sound silly and challenging, but my job as a professor is to get them to think, and college is a perfect time to question reality. The brains of college-aged students are developed enough to reflect and evaluate whether what they were previously told is accurate.

What we have been taught is *often not* accurate. Knowledge becomes outdated *constantly* and needs to be updated. That is the beauty and challenge of learning itself.

This has happened many times in history as knowledge ebbs and flows—yet somehow, it always comes as a shock. For example, the ancient Greeks in the third century B.C. knew the Earth was round. I was told my whole life that Europeans forgot this truth at some point, but then they discovered it was round *again* in 1492. I recently learned that Europeans did not *forget* the world was round but were debating about how big the Earth was. The fact that Europeans thought the world was flat for that long was a myth I believed until I was forty.

Likewise, Albert Einstein once said that his biggest blunder was that he knew the universe was expanding and possibly crunching. Still, because he could not see beyond a static universe, he changed his equations to reflect a static universe. Edwin Hubble later got the Nobel prize for "discovering" the expanding universe, which Einstein himself had discovered but disregarded. Hubble's real achievement was not the discovery itself but the ability to accept and embrace this discovery in place of the old.

Our misconceptions of race in this book are of the same caliber as these fundamental beliefs about our world. If we refuse to let discoveries shape us, we will make the same mistake as Einstein. We need to update the hardware that structures our society. Our programming is out of date. We need to reject outdated knowledge about race.

The information I was exposed to as a young adult radically challenged the beliefs and judgments I had been taught as a child. It challenged the narrative I held about myself and others who were different from me. I could have dismissed this new knowledge and hung on to my established and comfortable worldview. Instead, I let it reshape me—and it reshaped me for the better.

As you continue reading, I hope you will allow yourself to ask questions you may have never thought to ask before and challenge ideas that have seemed like a given for your entire life. I hope you will be free to see things anew and recognize myth from reality.

# CHAPTER 2

# The Inconsistency of Racial Categories

**I** **remember the first time** I had to teach the idea that nobody is *biologically* Black, White, Asian, Native American, Hispanic, etc. in a college classroom. It was one of the most awkward moments of my life. It was early in my teaching career. I was green, and the ideas I was about to present were new to me. I knew they would be new to the students as well.

I was nervous to give the lecture. In all my years of school, I had never heard anyone talk about the idea that nobody belongs to a race other than the human race. When I first learned about it, I thought I was the first to discover it, like Columbus. However, like Columbus, I was far from the first. There were many before me, like Charles Darwin and political scientist Wilbur Rich, who had already learned what I had learned.

Still, I was nervous about saying these words out loud. I knew it might stir issues—not from my dean, for they would have high-fived me and told me it is my job to have tough conversations to open minds. However, I knew there was a chance the students or parents may not respond well and that I could experience backlash. I needed to be prepared to support anything I said in the classroom from the critics, the naysayers, and the afraid.

I was especially conscious of this as I drove to teach that day as an adjunct in a rural area in the middle of Ohio. The college was close to the infamous billboards on Interstate 71 proclaiming "marriage is for a man and a woman" and the Ten Commandments. Let's say it's not the most liberal of towns.

I stood at the whiteboard in the middle of the room and looked at my group of about thirty-two students. It was an introduction to sociology class. I knew the students had never heard anything like what I was about to say. Most were White, with a few Black students and one Asian.

The room was set up like a baseball field, in which the professor stood at home plate, and the rest of the class was in the infield and the outfield. All the tables were curved in, so the students' eyes followed you like the Mona Lisa. I wore my typical shirt, loose tie, fancy pants, and a belt. I had recently shed the use of a full suit and shiny shoes, but I was still pretty preppy as I strode to the front and opened my notes for the day.

Scanning the curriculum book, I knew I would need to bypass all the sociological terms and explain this differently. From the front of the class, I closed the curriculum book and stood before them.

I said, "In the US, the dominant culture tells us that racial differences are facts, and they label us as belonging to a specific race. Raise your hand if you believe you belong to a race."

Every student tentatively raised their hand, clearly confused by my question.

I went on. "Right. Everyone. But let me ask you: have you ever questioned whether you are the race you are, or did you take people at their word when they informed you of your race? I mean, have you ever questioned whether you are biologically Black, White, Asian, Hispanic, Native American, etc.?"

Crickets. Some students kept their eyes on their books. Some shifted in their seats.

One student raised their hand and said, "Um, I've never thought about it."

I replied, "Well, that makes sense. Because we're not really taught to ask questions like that. We're just told what we are, who we are the same as, and who we are different from."

Another student in the front row raised their hand. "My parents are Black. My siblings are Black. My skin is Black. So, I don't really understand. Why would I wonder whether or not I'm Black?"

"That's exactly the point. You have been told you are Black, you identify as Black, and you have experienced life as Black. There are cultural experiences to being Black. But is there something in your *DNA* that makes you Black? That's the question I am encouraging us to ask."

I understood the confusion this young man was experiencing. And I've understood why some students bristle at the question. It can come across as affrontive to have someone call something as foundational as one's race into question—especially coming from someone categorized as a White male.

It can seem that I am invalidating their experiences, but that is not my purpose. My purpose is to get them to question what they have taken for granted and prompt them to reevaluate what they know based on science.

I continued, "Our ancestors come from different places, we look different, and we have different cultures. However, does that actually mean we are biologically different? Have you ever considered the idea that race, as a biological concept, doesn't really exist? What if I told you that race is just an idea that humans made up?"

The class was silent for a while longer. Even though I was a bit uncomfortable with it, I let the silence hang there. I wanted them to consider this idea. I must address these "radical" ideas in the classroom, or I would not be doing my job as a race and ethnicity professor.

Another student raised her hand to speak. She said, "My mom is White, and my dad is Black. So, I guess that makes me mixed race. But I've always felt confused about my race. When I fill out forms, sometimes I put White, or sometimes I put Black. I can pass for both. I never really know what to choose. When I visit my dad's family in Alabama, they call me Black. I always wonder, what does it matter? Or like, what exactly are they asking when they ask for my race? So … I know my parents are from different places and came from different cultures, but it kind of makes sense to me that the idea of race isn't as real as we've been told."

I have people who identify as mixed race in my classes all the time. Interestingly, they do not find these ideas affrontive. I can see how it opens doors for them. Qualitatively, mixed students may experience identity confusion because they do not know which race they belong to. I can see in mixed students' eyes that they find comfort in the fact that while they previously thought they were different because they were mixed, it turns out they are just like everybody else genetically, for all humans are incredibly mixed.

Many of my students from mixed heritage have an easier time seeing the truth beneath the categories we take for granted: our ideas about and categories of race are entirely arbitrary. These distinctions that generations have accepted as indisputable facts do not exist.

It takes a few weeks of discussing these ideas with my students before it starts to sink in that they are not biologically a member of any race except the human race. As their minds begin to open to new ideas, the first foundational idea we explore is that of a "social construct."

# Race As a Social Construct

If you were to step into a sociology classroom, "social construct" is likely one of the first phrases you'd hear being thrown around. A **social construct** is something humans create that does not exist in nature.

A social construct is not something like a tree because a tree's existence and basic properties can be proven through basic observation, regardless of what period, culture, or society you live in. A social construct is something like football. It is a game that does not exist in nature. We made the ball, the rules, the field, the fandoms—all of it.

Many of our ideas and conventions are not objective facts of reality. We are humans—it is in our nature to create things. And many things we have created are extraordinary—or at least neutral.

For example, the idea of Santa Claus is also a social construction. Santa Claus does not exist in nature. Humans came up with and spread the idea of Santa Claus. We have maintained the institution by socializing young children for generations to believe Santa Claus is real up to a certain age, even though we know it is just something we made up.

We all consciously understand that Santa Claus is not real. Still, there are plenty of other social constructs we think of as simply a part of life that are only real because we made them: holidays, traffic lights, the Constitution, and capitalism are all examples of social constructs. We make up holidays to celebrate, commemorate, and make meaning and traditions that color our lives. We socially construct new ones and deconstruct old ones all the time. Columbus Day is now Indigenous People's Day, Christmas used to be Yule, etc. Traffic lights are arbitrary lights in the sky that we were taught to recognize the meaning of and obey.

Similarly, the US Constitution was made up by a land-owning, American-born, European-descended elite who didn't want to pay taxes to England anymore. Capitalism is a modern invention that only recently came into play during the Industrial Revolution. These are all things we made up. They are all social constructions. Social constructions can be both material and non-material. They can be ideas, and they can be physical objects.

And, of course, some social constructs can be highly damaging. Think of DDT, microplastics, and nuclear weapons. None of these are naturally occurring scientific realities—they are simply a reflection and fabrication of our human nature's darker and apathetic parts.

Race is a social construct like this. "The social construction of race" is ultimately just a fancy sociological way of stating that the social world and its institutions, such as race, are created by us. There is no such thing as Black and White races in nature. Humans are the ones who created racial categories—meaning we all got together as a group and decided that races are real, and then we taught everyone about the idea we came up with.

Race is also one such social construct that has done an enormous amount of damage to humanity. Indeed, people have genetic and physical differences, but those differences do not align with our racial categories. In the next chapter, we will further explore how our idea of race came to be. But for now, please consider the arbitrary and shifting nature of the categories that most people go their whole lives without questioning.

## RACIAL CATEGORIES IN AMERICA

My own story and my students' stories call the objectivity of race into question. To call race even further into doubt, we only need to look at the nonsensical nature of racial categories themselves.

My friend Neil, whose parents migrated from India, described how, as a child, he would fill in "American Indian" on standardized tests or any place he had to check the "race" box. After all, he was Indian … and born in America—American Indian! Yet when he would tell others he was Indian, they would ask what tribe he was part of. Or teachers would correct him, saying, "You're not American Indian. You're Indian American."

Or sometimes, even more confusing to Neil, teachers might say, "No, you're Asian." Then, another person would come along and tell him he is not Asian because his family is from India—as if one needs to be from a specific set of countries on the continent of Asia to be considered "Asian."

Needless to say, Neil was confused about a lot of things, but he was right when he learned early on that our labels don't make any sense.

People may be ethnically different, but they are not different in a way that can be accurately codified by the US Census racial categories in use today. The US Census is the leading authority for counting and grouping every individual in the US. Many people don't realize that the Constitution legally mandates that the Census be used to measure demographics, including the racial composition of the US. While counting and codifying every person in the US is a vast undertaking, it was essential to the Founding Fathers that every person living in America belongs to a category and that the populations of those categories be closely monitored.

The first races recorded in 1790 by the US Census were "Slaves," "Free White Males and Females," and all "Other Free Persons." The categories were adjusted in the 1820 Census when "Free Colored Persons" was added. In the 1850 Census, the "Slaves" and "Free Colored Persons" categories were changed to "Black." "Mulatto" (Black and European) was also added. The "Free White" category was changed to "White."

Notice that the first categories Americans made were Black and White. Sociologist Jayne Ifekwunigwu explains, "The contemporary North American worldview on race emerged from a particular set of historical, economic, and political circumstances, including the subjugation of people of African descent during and after enslavement. This specific history explains why critical and popular US discourses on race predominantly pivot on a binary Black/White axis."[2] In other geopolitical contexts, the divisions stem from differences like color, caste, or social hierarchy. But in ours, the categories formed along the lines of color to

2    Jayne Ifekwunigwe et al., "A Qualitative Analysis of How Anthropologists Interpret the Race Construct," *American Anthropologist* 119, no. 3 (September 2009): 422. DOI: 10.1111/aman.12890.

explicitly delineate who was "free" and who was not.

In the 1860 Census, the first categories outside of "Black" or "White" were added: "Indian" and "Chinese." The categories were adjusted because patterns of immigration were increasing racial diversity, and Whites needed to distinguish further which races had liberty and which ones did not.

In the 1890 Census, "Japanese" was added to the "Chinese" category, and "Quadroon" (1/4 Black and 3/4 European) and "Octoroon" (1/8 Black) were added to the "Black; Mulatto" category. This was done to further distinguish which 'blended persons' were allowed rights and access and which ones did not. The lighter you were, the more access you could have. The darker you were, the less access you had.[3] In the 1900 Census, the "Black; Mulatto; Quadroon; Octoroon" category was condensed again to "Black (Negro); Mulatto." Also, an "Other" category was added for the first time.

The categories tell such a story. Through their lens, you can imagine how our nation changed in the generations following the initial founding. And you can nearly imagine the quandary of those in charge as more and more of the population defied the pre-established groupings.

During the twentieth century and into the twenty-first, racial categorization got really wild and was constantly in flux as America struggled to adjust to major social changes. For example, social movements led to new words like "African American" and "Native American." People from India became "Hindus" in 1930, but that category was removed, so they became "Asians,"

---

3   The range from light to dark is known as the color gradient, which is how race is measured in Latin America. In the US, we use racial categories, instead of categories along a color gradient.

then became "Asian Indians" in the 1990s, etc. Notice how much fluctuation follows.

Between 1930 and 2000, the "Black (Negro); Mulatto" category was changed to "Negro," then to "Negro or Black," then to "Black, African American, or Negro."

Groups lobbied to consolidate Latin Americans into a category eventually called "Hispanic." A "Mexican" category was added in 1930 but was removed in 1960. In 1970, a category was created called "Origin or Descent: Mexican; Puerto Rican, Cuban; Central or South American, Other Spanish." In 2000, it became "Spanish/Hispanic/Latino; Mexican, Mexican-American, Chicano; Puerto Rican; Cuban; Other Spanish/Hispanic/ Latino." Then, in 2010, it became "Hispanic, Latino, or Spanish Origin; Mexican, Mexican-American, Chicano; Puerto Rican; Cuban; Another Hispanic, Latino, or Spanish Origin."

For Asians and Pacific Islanders, in the 1920 Census, the "Chinese; Japanese" category was changed to "Chinese; Filipino; Hindu; Japanese; Korean." In 1950, it was changed to "Chinese; Filipino; Japanese." In 1960, it became "Chinese; Filipino; Japanese" and added back in "Korean." In 1970, it was changed to "Asian Indian; Chinese; Filipino; Japanese; Korean; Vietnamese." In 1990, it changed to "Asian or Pacific Islander; Chinese; Filipino; Korean, Japanese; Vietnamese; Asian Indian; other API." In 2000, it became "Asian Indian; Chinese; Filipino; Japanese; Korean; Vietnamese; Other Asian."

For Hawaiians and Pacific Islanders, in 1960, a "Hawaiian: Part Hawaiian" category was created. In 1970, it was simplified to "Hawaiian." In 1980, it became "Hawaiian; Guamanian; Samoan." In 1990, "Other API" was added to "Hawaiian; Guamanian; Samoan." In 2000, it became "Native Hawaiian; Guamanian or Chamorro; Samoan; Other Pacific Islander."

The category for Native Americans has also fluctuated for decades. In the 1960 Census, "Indian" was changed to "Aleut; American Indian, Eskimo." Then, in the 1970 Census, the title became "Indian (American)." In the 1980 Census, "Indian (American)" was changed to "Aleut; Eskimo; Indian (American)." In the 2000 Census, it became "American Indian or Alaska Native."

In 2000, the "Other" category was changed to "Some Other Race."

In the 2020 Census, *all* the old categories were thrown out the window, and new ones were constructed, stating that Hispanic is to be considered an ethnicity, not a race. So, the new racial categories used in the 2020 Census are as follows: "Hispanic," "White alone, non-Hispanic," "Black or African American alone, non-Hispanic," "Asian alone, non-Hispanic," "American Indian and Alaska Native alone, non-Hispanic," "Native Hawaiian and Other Pacific Islander alone, non-Hispanic," "Multiracial, non-Hispanic," and "Some Other Race alone, non-Hispanic."

Furthermore, it became trickier to measure race because the US Census asks whether you are Hispanic and what race you are in another question. Plus, it asks you both questions, which again blends race and ethnicity into a single category even though they are separate constructs. On top of that, it is also confusing because if you are Hispanic and from Latin America and you answer "yes" to the Hispanic question, then what race should you check in the following box when the only options are White, Black, American Indian or Alaska Native, a bunch of checkboxes for different countries in Asia, and Some Other Race? Are Latin Americans also "Some Other Race," according to the US Census in 2020? It is so confusing.

The history of US Census racial categories is a fascinating historical record that shows how the country has expanded and diversified and how those in power have attempted to make sense of and categorize the identities of these diverse populations.

The only category that has not experienced severe fluctuation is—you guessed it!—White. It was initially "Free White," and then it became "White" in 1850. It has not changed since. It has remained a stable, protective status while all manner of other categories have been created to essentially identify and organize the non-White population.

Another notable observation from this record is that the Census has always struggled to categorize mixed races. It simply categorizes people according to country of origin, an attribute of ethnicity, and self-identification. Yet statistics show that in the last ten years since the US Census has recorded their data and added more racial categories, four times as many people identify as more than one race.[4]

There are other great untold or near-forgotten stories of racial mixing in America that we don't have categories for. What race is an Asian Mexican, a Hawaiian Asian Indian, or a Black Native American? What words do we know in our vernacular to identify their racial category? There are no words for these blends that have existed in the US for centuries. I have no idea what to call an Asian Mexican. They are "Other Race," according to the US Census.

Our ability to constantly reconstruct racial categories to fit our needs illuminates how they are not universal. They are social constructions. We created them, and we continue to recreate them. This also means we can change them.

---

4    Kim Parker et al., *Multiracial in America: Proud, Diverse, and Growing in Numbers* (Pew Research Center, 2015), 1.

Clearly, these categories are not even genuinely objective or universal within our own country and systems. Instead, they reflect how we draw and continuously redraw the lines that separate us.

## RACIAL CATEGORIES AROUND THE WORLD

In the US, knowing what race you belong to can be confusing. Simply understanding the categories can be confusing, like the fact that people from most of Africa are categorized as Black, but those from *North* Africa are classified as White. Furthermore, the racial categories we tend to accept as an objective reality in the US are not even used in most other countries around the world. In fact, not all countries use race as the basis for grouping people.

For example, in Latin America, classification is based on the color gradient, which measures a person's race along a spectrum from light to dark skin color. As a result, there are racial categories you have probably never heard of, such as Branco (White), Pardo (brown), Preto (Black), Amarelo (Asian), Indígena (indigenous), Moreno (brown), Moreno Claro (light brown), Negro (Black), and Claro (light brown). Interestingly, "mestizo" also has a different meaning in Latin America than in the United States. In the US, it means European mixed with Native American. In Latin America, it means an American with pure European ancestry.

Conversely, in Singapore, groups are categorized according to blood purity. The scale is not about skin color but about how Chinese or non-Chinese you are. For example, within the Singaporean racial framework, there is one racial group called Peranakan, which indicates a hybrid of Chinese, Indonesian, Western, and Malay identities. They have a variety of particular racial categories that rule their society just as tangibly as our society reflects our ideas about race—but the lines are drawn in completely different places.

I love teaching at a particular nursing college I work at. Most students there are from Africa, Latin America, or anywhere not in the United States. I do qualitative surveys with them every semester and ask them, for example, "When did you find out you were Black?" At first, this may sound like a silly question, but to someone from Africa, it makes complete sense because they didn't know they were Black until they came to America and they were called "Black" for the first time.

Each country and culture has its unique way of dividing society—sometimes by race, cultural traits, religion, status, or region. These are all social constructs we have created and perpetuate as we live by them.

# CHAPTER 3

# The Origins of the Race Myth

**I**f we take the time to think critically about our racial categories, the fact that race is not an inherent, fixed truth is not as surprising as it may have initially seemed. The way scholars Audrey and Brian Smedley put it, "From its inception, race was a folk idea, a culturally invented conception about human differences."[5] We see this sentiment resonate across our lived experience and history.

The word "race" itself has been used to categorize people for thousands of years in different ways. For example, my wife did not know she was "White" until she moved from Albania to America as a child. In her country of origin, racism is not between people of different skin colors but between people of other cultures. Specifically, Western Balkan history tends to be full of

---

5   Audrey Smedley, Brian Smedley, "Race as Biology is Fiction, Racism as a Social Problem is Real: Anthropological and Historical Perspectives on the Social Construction of Race," *American Psychologist* 60, no. 1 (January 2005): 22. DOI: 10.1037/0003-066X.60.1.16.

stigma towards Roma people—whom most Albanians consider to be a different "race" even though they would be regarded as the same race by American categories. Shakespeare used the word "race" to categorize a group of bishops as a "race" of bishops. The rules around the word have always been murky.

However, the use of race to categorize people along a Black-White axis is a new use of the word when the span of human history is considered. How did we develop this idea that we needed to categorize people by obscure and inaccurate features and supposed biology? This chapter will further unpack how we got to our divisive place.

Before the 1700s, race was traditionally used more like ethnicity in modern times. Classical races generally refer to groups from a specific country or culture. For example, the Romans and Greeks considered each other different races, even though we may find that ridiculous in modern times because the countries are so close. As another example, the Chinese considered light-skinned people Barbarians, even though this category referred to non-Han people living outside the heartland with a different way of life—not people of a different race in the way we typically think of it.

The idea that physical traits are associated with how "evolved" or "superior" groups are goes back thousands of years. The Greeks thought that people who grew up in extreme climates were evolutionarily tougher than people who grew up in mild climates. The Romans considered the Celts and Germanic people a tough race and accounted for this due to their upbringing in rugged mountainous regions. Seventh-century Christians and Muslims thought that people with black skin were a cursed race, descended from a cursed man named Ham. They used this supposed curse as a justification for the Trans-Atlantic Slave Trade.

During the Enlightenment, philosophers and scientists applied logic to observing human differences. They assumed it was logical that people with different skin colors from various countries were biologically separate from each other along the same lines. The adage that some groups evolved separately (and more so) than others reared its ugly head. This became the foundation of scientific racism, in which European descendants attempted to prove that they were superior to other people.

This was an illogical leap for an age of supposed logic, considering that Europe is not its own continent—it is part of Eurasia and extremely close to Africa. Of course, Europeans did not evolve in isolation, let alone superiority to other people groups. In addition, in the 1860s, Charles Darwin made it quite clear from his discoveries that physical traits were irrelevant as measures of racial categories and that all humans were on equal footing regarding intelligence. However, this knowledge from Charles Darwin never became common knowledge in the culture. This knowledge did not particularly benefit those who had the power to disseminate it.

As a result, in the 1750s, the categorization of the human species into five races that could be hierarchically ranked from superior to inferior became popular. By 1790, the US Census had firmly established racial categories as a demographic reality. Throughout the 18th, 19th, and 20th centuries, racial anthropology (often known as scientific racism) was applied to justify racist ideology and eugenics.

# The Language of Division in America

Of course, there were many grounds for division before the creation of America. But the birth of America infused the prejudiced preconceptions that came before it into this new and experimental social context.

When I teach race and ethnicity, I always tell my students this is a "thinking class." I teach them that the goal of this class is to learn a way of thinking about race and ethnicity and how they developed. I always make them start with some basic history and then explain the association between race and social class in America in their own words. When they can do that, I know they get it, and my job here is done. Here is the history my classes learn.

During the Age of Colonialism, Europeans set out to explore the globe. They took over various societies in India, Australasia, the Americas, and parts of Africa and Asia. They explored the North and South Poles. They were everywhere, engaging in global trade to expand profits during the rise of capitalism.

When the Europeans arrived in the Americas, they had a chance to make friends, but instead, they made war. They conquered and usurped in accordance with the American notion of manifest destiny. They conquered territories violently and drew lines on maps to represent their conquered lands, many of which still represent most of the country borders in use today.[6] Over time, they began establishing themselves in these conquered lands in what became called colonies. In these colonies, they imposed their economic and cultural way of life upon the subjects.

Whose fault it is that the war between the Natives and

---

6    Prior to the Age of Colonialism, the US did not even exist on European maps.

Europeans occurred is an interesting question, one that brings you down the rabbit hole of whether the decimation of 95% of Native Americans was war or genocide, for example. One way to view it is that the Natives lost the battle. Another is that we took their land. The British did not consider all the Native Americans dying to be a genocide. It was manifest destiny to them, as it was to the Founding Fathers. But, in modern times, we often perceive it as genocide because it was.

Europeans spread capitalism as they crisscrossed the planet. Christopher Columbus made clear his intentions to enslave and exploit for profit in his notes.[7] Everywhere they went, Europeans developed a social context in which inequality was pervasive so they could consolidate capital into the hands of the few. For example, Belgium was built on the backs of Congolese laborers (see King Leopold's Ghost by Adam Hochschild). The elite Europeans and their descendants became the world's bourgeoisie, reaping illustrious privilege while the masses labored away.

Europeans built a capitalist social system that required exploitable labor so that the capitalists could profit from the goods and services provided. To support this system, they wanted to create a social system (e.g., a capitalist class system) in which they could protect their domination. For that to happen, they first needed a way to know who was allowed to have a chance to rise and who was to be blocked access. This required the distinction between a ruling class and a laboring class.

There were not enough poor Whites to exploit, so Europeans turned to slavery to fill a void. Enslaved people were needed in the Americas to have an exploitable lower-class workforce by which the bourgeoisie could profit from the use of cheap labor.

---

7    Library of Congress, *Exploring the Early Americas: Columbus and Taino* (2025).

Europeans needed backs to labor in the fields and dig the silver and gold out of the rocks.

Hence, during the 1700s, there was a need to determine who the enslaved people would be. Who was "different" enough from them? There were the Irish, whom the British were willing to enslave, except for the fact that the British considered the Irish too lazy. The Native Americans were good candidates, but there were very few left, so the Europeans worked the remaining local Native Americans to death in the silver mines.

Who was left then? Africans. The slave trade had existed in Africa for thousands of years, but the Europeans made it big business. They created the Trans-Atlantic slave trade. Europeans bought enslaved people from Africa and sent them to cotton fields and sugar plantations controlled by European powers. In these colonies, those enslaved also built the roads, the buildings, and essentially the entire infrastructure Whites depended upon for profit. The Dutch brought the first enslaved people to the Americas in 1652. The Swedes, English, French, and Spanish all followed suit.

The English made slavery a corporation. They had approximately one hundred and fifty slave ships, each carrying tens of thousands of people. Over an estimated twelve million enslaved people were brought to the Americas. Between the mid-1600s and the late 1800s, three-quarters of the US population were enslaved. The rest were "Free White Males and Females." Enslaved Americans were stripped of liberty and freedom, along with their culture and their families. They were offered for sale and purchased in stores. They were given new names and often compelled to convert to Christianity.

Slavery was justified by legal institutions that supported the practice. After all, that was precisely the design of this capitalist system: to give "the few" power to run the country how they pleased.

Now, all they needed was language to reflect and solidify this institution. They went based on the most immediately identifiable factor: skin color. They came up with the words "White" and "Slave/Black." The concept of being "White," therefore, came from a need for Europeans to demarcate the powerful from the powerless.

The creation of racial categories enabled Europeans to remove competition from the economic and social arenas. Thanks to this change, all minority races were restricted from having access to compete with Whites for socioeconomic status. Women were already prohibited from competing globally; thus, half of the competition was removed. By creating racial categories, Europeans could further remove competition, enabling them to consolidate capital into the hands of the few more easily. Essentially, for most of the history of the US, only White males could compete for power.

While race originated along a Black-White axis, Whites historically placed themselves on top of the social hierarchy of all countries they conquered. In those conquered lands, non-Europeans, who later became labeled as non-Whites (e.g., Black, Asian, Native American, Hispanic, etc.), were subjugated to the bottom of the class system as well.

Europeans achieved their elite status through violence, oppression, and by building a prejudicial and discriminatory social system that privileged White males. The blocking of access for all racial minorities was supported legally and by social norms.

# The Creation of an "Elite" Class

In formal terms, this is how racial categories originated, and all of us ended up belonging to a racial group: Europeans socially constructed races to stratify society into socioeconomic groups so that capitalist European males could consolidate power into the hands of the few. Europeans created racial categories to establish a clear-cut dividing line between social classes. This is the association between race and social class: one's race historically dictated one's social class location in the hierarchically stratified social system.

A social system structured by slavery is the ultimate form of subjugation, even more so than a caste system, in which social mobility is nearly impossible. To enslave someone requires dehumanizing them to control them. Enslaved Africans were seen as beasts or animals, not humans. There are stories of plantation owners who said they never thought of their slaves as people until they became Christians. The hypocrisy of humans dehumanizing other humans is a struggle to cope with for myself and my co-author. Still, it is something we must face to understand the origin of racism.

If you still find it challenging to grasp the idea that racial categories were only created to separate the "elite" class from the others, consider the following stories.

In the 1920s, the US banned South Asians from naturalizing as US citizens. They also revoked the citizenship of existing naturalized South Asians on the premise that Hindus were too "brunette" to be considered American. ("Brunette" was a was a very loose term at the time.)

One of the many people affected by these laws was Bhagat Singh Thind, who was from Taragarh, India.[8] He did not feel this was right, especially after Thind served in World War I. As an Indian diaspora writer and lecturer, he later wrote and spoke about his experience and the unexpected move he made next: he petitioned the Supreme Court that he should be granted citizenship based on his Caucasian ancestry.

The Supreme Court was confused by his petition. After all, he was from India. But Thind argued that the original Aryans came from modern-day northwest India and Pakistan. The original Caucasians were people from the Caucasus region, which ranges between the Caspian and Black Seas along the border of Persia and India. Aryans come from northwest India, but the groups blended due to proximity. He argued that, based on historical evidence, South Asians are descended from Aryans blended with Caucasians. (Had the Nazis not spent so much time burning books but instead read books, they would have discovered that their "precious" Aryan race originated in northwest India.)

Thind's request was denied on the basis that "his type of Caucasian" wasn't the "European kind of Caucasian" and was not what the founders intended when they granted Caucasians citizenship. To be White or Caucasian meant to be from Europe, according to the Supreme Court, even though Caucasians did not even originate in Europe.

Thind's argument was based on logic and historical accuracy, but both were disregarded. This further proved that the categories were not built to support either logic or historical accuracy.

8    Doug Coulson, "British Imperialism, the Indian Independence Movement, and the Racial Eligibility Provisions of the Naturalization Act: United States v. Thind Revisited," *Georgetown Journal of Law & Modern Critical Race Perspectives* 7 (May 2015): 1–42. SSRN: https://ssrn.com/abstract=2610266.

They were designed to protect the power of a specific and prede-termined group of people.

Similarly, a Japanese person, Takao Ozawa, was barred from citizenship under the same law. In 1922, he applied to the Supreme Court, arguing that his skin color was as white as White people's skin color and that he should be allowed to be a citizen based on this.

Ozawa's physical whiteness was deemed insufficient, can-celed out by his Japanese (not European) descent. This meant that even having white skin didn't make you White.

Again, Ozawa's argument was based on another logical an-gle. And again, the Supreme Court's design upheld the truth that the categories were not built on this type of logic either. Ozawa received no explanation other than that he was not the right type of White. He was not part of the specific population that those in power deemed the ruling class. Ultimately, these stories serve to once again reveal the truth that any basis presented for race always leads back to a logical fallacy. The lines were not drawn along logic. The lines were drawn to establish insiders.

# Racism As a Societal Pillar

I love America. I am proud to be an American. This book is not meant as a platform to put down America. One reason my co-author and I wrote this book was to make the future better for Americans. But to think of racism spreading over time across this country is a misunderstanding. America was *built* on rac-ism. Racism was written into the Constitution. Racism is a pillar of American society. As America grew, racism grew, and it has not gone away.

Black and other non-White people were historically denied fundamental rights. They were considered three-fifths of a person in the Constitution solely for the benefit of slave-owning states to have a larger population and, therefore, more control of political power. Black people, themselves, were not considered citizens or had any rights. When rights were finally granted with the 14th Amendment, Jim Crow Laws were enacted to suppress minority races from participating in society. Lynching was also heavily utilized during Jim Crow as a means for Whites to control the Black population. Entire towns turned violent to suppress the rise of Black individuals, such as with the murderous Whites of Wilmington, North Carolina, in 1898.

The Chinese Exclusion Act barred Asians from becoming US citizens. The Japanese were interned. The Indian Removal Act of 1830 led to the Trail of Tears. Plessy vs Ferguson legalized segregation. The US was so antisemitic before World War II that even though the US government knew Jewish people were being murdered, they still denied them sanctuary and sent the boats back to Europe to die. The list goes on regarding how US law has been applied to support legalized racism.

The denial of fundamental rights is what enabled Whites to dominate society while all other groups were subjugated to the lower classes. Slavery may be the origin of institutional racism, but across all institutions, racist ideologies and policies were implemented to keep non-whites down. Racial minorities were denied access to becoming doctors and lawyers. They weren't allowed to marry someone that was White. Getting enough money to buy a house was nearly impossible.

All this to say, we do not live in a fair or meritocratic society. Every person does not have an equal chance. Some have **ascribed**

**status** (which you are born with), and some have **achieved status** (which you earn through work). Some have both, and some have no status through either. Meritocracy, the idea that we can move up the social class ladder based on talent and hard work, is an ideal—but not an American reality. We can live in denial and pretend that race (along with biological sex, gender, sexual orientation, religion, disability status, age, attractiveness, country of origin, etc.) does not structure our cultural way of life and our ability to ascend the social class ladder, but that would be ignorant.

There are structures in society that institutionally privilege groups of people. Race is one of those institutions that enables people to be excluded from society. This is the truth of its origin: it was simply a tool borrowed from generations past to implement a new system of inequality based on what the founders saw as the blank canvas of American society.

# CHAPTER 4

# What Science Says About Race

The idea of race as a biological reality is one of the most pervasive myths in our human history. The creation of racial groups has always been motivated by the desire to separate those who have power from those who do not.

Plenty of "scientific" explanations have been proposed to justify these categories. To modern ears, some are obviously false—like the idea that the shape of someone's skull could determine their personality and morality.

I first heard about this "scientific" claim, called phrenology, in high school. I was in an AP Psychology class, and the teacher told the class about the history of psychology and how psychologists had spent a long time measuring skulls to find evidence that Europeans were different from other races. This false notion about skulls was accepted as common knowledge for centuries and became embedded in Victorian society's cultural understanding of race.

Even though we have since disproved the idea that skull size is associated with race and morality, most people are still aware this idea existed. I remember being shocked at the time that people truly believed that. However, many scientific myths still ground our understanding of the world and race today, even though they have been disproved. This chapter will cover some of the most common scientific myths underpinning our race categories.

# Myth 1: Race is based on geography.

I was always told I was different from someone who grew up on a different continent. From all my years of teaching this subject, I've seen that most people also think this to be true.

This idea goes back thousands of years. On any map made before the 1700s, everything is skewed. Not all land masses had been discovered at that time. Antarctica wasn't discovered until 1820. When people looked at the maps, they decided there were about seven continents. This was widespread knowledge until the 1960s and taught in schools ubiquitously through the 1980s. It is still often taught in modern times.

It was not a far leap from looking at a map and then looking at people from different places on that map and simply assuming that because they look different from you, they are different. Historically, people thought others from distant lands were, in a way, "alien." Evidence of this can be seen in how some would put people from Africa on display in zoos in the early twentieth century and portray them as subhuman. In modern times, we still refer to immigrants as aliens. This may be stigmatic now, but the "illegal alien" concept lingers in our lexicon.

Granted, people from around the globe often bear significant physical differences. These are the visible characteristics of
someone's genotype interacting with their environment. You can
look at peoples' hair from different continents and see apparent
differences. Skin color variations depend on where one is born
on this Earth.

For all these makers of difference, it made logical sense to
people hundreds of years ago when they assumed that people
from different continents are fundamentally different. Thus,
based upon the early notion of seven continents and the idea
that people living on other continents were distinct, we came to
believe that people from various continents are biologically different in the form of races.

# Truth 1: Race is not based on geography.

Much of the foundation of racist ideology is based upon the false
idea that people from different continents are different on a biological level—a different type of human altogether.

The idea that racial groups evolved separately based on the
continent of their ancestors is built on the idea that continents
are separate entities. This supported the idea that Europeans and
Africans somehow evolved into different strains of humanity due
to isolation.

However, in the 1960s, scientists discovered that the Earth's
crust consists of tectonic plates. They saw that separate continents exist, but not with the dividing lines we imagined. When I
found out there are closer to fourteen tectonic plates (continents)
and Europe is not separate from Asia, essentially meaning that

Asians and Europeans live on the same continent, I was dumb-founded and forced to rethink everything I ever knew to be true.

We now know that Europe and Asia are not separate entities but one big continent. Therefore, Europe is not actually on its own continent but part of a single continent called Eurasia.

You might think, "Sure, they may be the same continent. But people were still separated by significant divides like mountains, oceans, rivers, etc., that could have made them developmentally different." And yes, we know that epigenetic factors like climate, region, parentage, and diet cause people to develop different physical traits.

However, geographical obstacles by no means kept people isolated into separate groups throughout history. Over time, natural obstacles *could* have blocked us from mixing if we weren't, as a species, so excellent at getting around and terraforming the planet. However, we do get around, and we mix as we go. According to more recent studies, we now know that "Europe was repopulated several times, as groups from various points in Central Asia and the Middle East displaced the existing populations. What we think of as European Whites are indeed an amalgam. So are today's East Asians, South Asians, sub-Saharan Africans, and Amerindians. Ancestral populations did not evolve quietly in isolation. Genetic ancestry is endlessly fluid and dynamic."[9]

Europeans spread their DNA like all the other conquering nations and traversing people have done for thousands of years. We have crisscrossed the planet during past epochs through the present, mixing DNA all the way. The oceans were crossed long before Columbus sailed the ocean blue. He gets all the credit,

___
9    Charles Murray, *Human Diversity: The Biology of Gender, Race, and Class* (New York City: Twelve, 2020), 148.

even though the Vikings did it a thousand years before, and Polynesians island-hopped across the South Pacific to Hawaii long before the Vikings made their voyages. People crossed the Bering Strait from Asia to North America and South America. Africans have sailed to Latin America and vice versa for thousands of years before the Vikings crossed the Atlantic. For evidence of this, examine ancient boat-building technology across continents. You will find that West Coast Africans and Native Americans in the Pacific Northwest built dug-out boats nearly the same way.[10]

Have you ever looked at how close Africa is to European countries, like Spain, France, Italy, and Greece on an accurate map? Not the maps in school. Those maps always make Europe look way larger and Africa way smaller than they are. You need an accurate map showing the truth: Africa is huge, and Europe is tiny. A quick boat ride or a two-day walk, and you can travel from Europe to Africa and vice versa. Morocco and Spain can kiss each other across the Strait of Gibraltar. Europeans have conquered African countries, and Africans have conquered European countries. People from the Middle East conquered both and have been conquered by both. The Carthaginian general Hannibal rode elephants from Africa to Europe. Alexander the Great traveled by foot to India. Genghis Khan rode horses from East Asia to Europe. Humans have been mixing, mixing, and mixing as the planet's population has exponentially grown.

Why did Europeans think they were a separate and superior race that evolved beyond that of other races when humans have been blending throughout our entire history? Europeans are essentially next-door neighbors to Africans, Middle Easterners,

---

10    Abubakar Garba, "The Architecture and Chemistry of a Dug-Out: The Dufuna Canoe," *Ethno-Archaeological Perspective* (1996), 193–200.

and Asians. They have been mixing genes for thousands of years, in brothels, across the silk road, through rape and pillaging, through marriage and consent. Nobody is "pure-blooded" from *any* particular location. Essentially, we are all "Some Other Race."

This is what it means to say that no continental clusters of races exist. Continents are not barriers to humans. We have been crossing them for thousands of years. "The idea that humans can be divided biologically by large continental clusters that have been defined by geographic barriers (the so-called SHO theory, which stands for Sahara, Himalayan, Ocean) has been thoroughly disproven by geneticists."[11] To assume that any group evolved separately from the rest of humanity is false.

# Myth 2: Race is divided by physical features.

Our brains naturally notice differences. They can tell that someone has a different skin color, nose shape, or hair than you. We humans decided what these differences would *mean* for us as a society.

Of course, skin color is the most historically significant marker used to define race. For generations, children have been socialized to associate darker skin color with inferiority and lighter skin color with beauty and prestige. We have also structured our society upon the idea that skin color means something.

---

11    Javier Perez-Rodriguez, Alejandro de la Fuente, "Now Is the Time for a Postracial Medicine: Biomedical Research, the National Institutes of Health, and the Perpetuation of Scientific Racism," *American Journal of Bioethics* 17, no. 9 (September 2017): 36–47. DOI: 10.1080/15265161.2017.1353165.

Hair texture and eye shape have also been used as markers of race. As a society, we have perpetuated the idea that arbitrary differences like these carry some deeper meaning about how much we have in common with someone.

# Truth 2: Similar appearances do not reflect similar DNA.

Physical appearances like blue eyes, curly hair, or skin color are phenotypes. A **phenotype** results when our genotype interacts with our environment and manifests as a physical trait you can observe with your eyes. Genetics influences phenotypes, and we can see this when a child inherits physical characteristics from their parents.

However, phenotypes are not entirely genetic—environmental factors also influence them. Just because people look alike does not mean they share common genetics. Due to the complex intermixing of humanity for thousands of years, compounded by evolutionary selection pressures, the effect of genes upon phenotypes is diverse across all human groups[12]. This is why some Black people have light skin, some dark. Some White people look Latin, and some Latin people look African. My wife always says her father looks Asian, though he was born in Albania.

How we categorize others by appearance is often inaccurate, but even more to the point: how we categorize ourselves is typically not even accurate! Racial categories and self-reported racial identification usually do not match genetic ancestry. If we've

---

12   Lian Deng, Shuhua Xu, "Adaptation of Human Skin Color in Various Populations," *Hereditas* 155, no. 1 (2018): 1. https://doi.org/10.1186/s41065-017-0036-2.

learned anything from the ancestry DNA testing craze in recent years, it's this! For example, African Americans self-reporting as Black often have up to 99% European ancestry; those identifying as White often have a blend of African and European; Mexican Americans generally have around 3% African ancestry; 16% of Puerto Ricans have African ancestry.[13] What you see on the outside is not always what is happening on the inside. Hence, again, our eyes and logic often deceive us.

Therefore, to assume people who look similar have similar genetics is just as false as our racial categories based on continental clusters.

# Myth 3: Race is divided by common DNA.

It made logical sense to people in the past that the racial categories they created accurately categorized people according to biological differences between groups. The creators of the racial groups we use today did not have genetic testing at their fingertips. They assumed that people of different skin colors from various countries were different, and we continue to believe this today: even if race is not marked by location or appearance, some genetic commonality links us with "our people" and separates us from others.

---

13    Tesfaye B Mersha, Tilahun Abebe, "Self-reported race/ethnicity in the age of genomic research: its potential impact on understanding health disparities," *Human Genomics* 9, no. 1 (January 2015): 1. https://doi.org/10.1186/s40246-014-0023-x.

# Truth 3: Racial categories do not accurately group people according to common DNA.

Genetic studies show that humanity shares over 99.9% of their DNA. Genetically, we are overwhelmingly similar to any given person on the globe, no matter how distinct we look or how different our backgrounds are. We now know there are no statistically significant clusters of common DNA separated by country of origin or physical trait.[14]

The following research findings are from a researcher at the College of Charleston named Erik Sotka. His conclusions challenge all our common assumptions in an enlightening way:

1. Of the genome of any two humans, 99.5–99.9% is identical. Single nucleotide diversity accounts for 0.1% of the variation, while structural variations accounts for the remaining 0.4%. This degree of diversity is quite low, compared to other species, and is related to the relatively short time of human existence on Earth, along with our capability to cross physical barriers and extensive genetic admixture.

2. Out of the 0.1–0.5% variation between any two unrelated individuals, the largest amount of variation, 85%, is between individuals within the same local population.

3. Genetic variation is complex, multidirectional, and continuous ("clinal") throughout the world, without gaps or sharp boundaries. Some populations in Sub-Saharan Africa are more genetically similar to European populations than to other Sub-Saharan African populations.

---

14    Erik Sotka, "Clines," *Encyclopedia of Ecology*, 2nd ed. (2008): 26–31.

4. There are no identifiable continental genomic clusters.

5. Allelic clusters exist throughout the world. However, these are usually small and not representative of large populations, particularly not continental populations. These clusters may be the result of evolutionary phenomena such as the combination of founder or bottleneck effects with endogamy.

To be truly genetically distinct from someone else, there have to be enough allele differences between two peoples' chromosomes. An **allele** is a form of a gene that codes for a specific trait. However, humans do not tend to have significant variations of alleles in our DNA compared to each other.

For instance, a single African individual may be just as genetically different from another African as they are from someone elsewhere in the world. Yet, all humans are equally similar when looking at populations as a whole.

The only way meaningful genetic variation occurs is if a group evolved in complete isolation in modern times, which is rare. For example, there *are* groups in the highlands that have historically been more adapted to elevation changes. This is reflected in their DNA through allele differences that vary compared to most humans across the planet. However, due to globalization, unique DNA on a group level is incredibly rare.

Let's say we wanted to create *accurate* categories for that.1% of genetic diversity from one another. The 0.1%–0.5% genetic difference among humans arises through natural selection in response to specific local environments. This explains why some people can digest milk (as seen in populations from Ethiopia to Europe), why some individuals develop asthma, how skin tone adapts to different climates, and why some groups share genetic resistance to diseases like malaria.

Every person is genetically unique. However, at the population level, these individual differences do not neatly fit into racial categories like the ones used in the US today. To truly capture genetic diversity, we would need thousands of categories, as broad racial labels fail to reflect the complexity of human variation.

For this reason, biomedicine has a great debate regarding whether race should be used in the medical community. When examining disease prevalence, for example, racial differences seem to stand out in the data. Often, we hear of things like certain types of breast cancers being more prevalent in certain races. For example, TNBC (triple negative breast cancer) was thought to be more common for African American females in the past.

However, when socioeconomic status was controlled for, racial differences for that type of breast cancer were not significant, suggesting that the social context, such as lack of resources, accounted for disparities between groups, not biological differences between races. The researchers found that as socioeconomic status decreased, TNBC rates increased. Belonging to a minority race is associated with a reduction in health quality and access due to environmental and socioeconomic effects resulting from marginalization, *not* their racial biology.

The medical community is adjusting to the idea that self-identified race or the use of US-Census-approved social categories cannot predict genotype or drug responses, for example. Using race as a guide for how to treat patients oversimplifies the role that ancestry and health play. The association between race and disease has only spurious associations. A better way to use race for the medical community would be to individually test a person's genes and compare it to genetics with similar markings.

This truth is summarized well by American anthropologist Audrey Smedley:

Anthropologists and biologists no longer see 'races' as discrete populations defined by blood-group patterns or 'types' defined by averages of statistical measurements. Biophysical variations are seen as continuous and gradual, overlapping population boundaries, fluid, and subject to evolutionary changes. In like manner, scholars honestly examining the history of American attitudes toward human differences have concluded that 'race' was a social invention of the eighteenth century that took advantage of the superficial physical differences among the American population and the social roles that these people played and transposed these into a new form of social stratification.[15]

The social stratification Smedley describes is precisely correct: these groupings only serve to fragment society on arbitrary lines. And even when used in the most well-meaning ways, like to help medical populations, they only result in further and often dire miscalculations.

# Myth 4: One race can be genetically inferior or superior to another.

For years, scientists attempted to prove that one race was genetically superior to another, but their efforts consistently failed. One well-documented example of this so-called "scientific racism" is Thomas Jefferson, who argued that slavery was justifiable because

---

15    Audrey Smedley, ""Race" and the Construction of Human Identity," *American Anthropologist* 100, no. 3 (September 1998): 690–702. https://doi.org/10.1525/aa.1998.100.3.690.

Black people were naturally inferior. He was not alone in this belief. Many nineteenth-century scientists, including Samuel G. Morton, Josiah Clark Nott, and Samuel Cartwright, gained recognition by publishing studies—using what they claimed were rigorous scientific methods. With these studies, they attempted to demonstrate White superiority in intelligence and other traits.

Theodore Roosevelt was another prominent supporter of eugenics, a movement that gained significant traction in the first half of the twentieth century. In the United States, public health officials actively endorsed eugenics-based policies, leading to forced sterilizations and efforts to control birth rates and immigration. Laws were passed with the intent of "improving" society based on these ideas. Some individuals took these beliefs to extreme and horrifying levels. For instance, William Hornaday, a once-respected zoologist and director of the New York Zoological Park, placed a Congolese man, Ota Benga—who was likely kidnapped—on display in the zoo's Monkey House in 1906, with the approval of the New York Zoological Society.

The impact of eugenics extended beyond the US. The Nazi regime in Germany modeled some of its racial policies on California's eugenics laws. However, after the devastation of World War II—marked by genocide and the loss of over 50 million lives—scientific racism and eugenics largely fell out of favor. Still, the idea of biological races persisted, leaving a troubling legacy that we must confront and reconcile with today.[16] This is the past we are left to reconcile with.

---

16    Perez-Rodriguez and de la Fuente, 37.

# Truth 4: No racial group can claim genetic superiority.

People with certain genetic traits can indeed be better suited to specific skills. For example, someone with a height advantage may be better at basketball or volleyball than someone shorter (though this is not always true). Regardless, just because someone is tall and someone else is short does not mean they are different types of humans on a biological level or separate races with other DNA.

Scientific racism has been disproven time and time again. For example, scientists in the past spuriously found that African Americans were inferior in intelligence compared to Europeans. In the early 20th century, American psychologists used the Stanford-Binet intelligence test results as evidence that one race was more intelligent than another. However, the psychologists did not consider the actual variables that play a role, such as socioeconomic status. When you put an entire race in poverty and restrict their access to quality education, how well are they going to do on a test that requires formal education to score highly? Misleading and biased scientific evidence was used heavily in the nineteenth and early twentieth centuries to support the idea that non-Whites were primitive humans.[17]

Despite years of efforts to prove otherwise, we know intelligence is not associated with race. Studies have found that differences in measures of success, like intellect, can be attributed to other causes, but not race. Other causes include cultural segregation and access to resources. These can also include poverty and parent's genetics. (Parents' genetics being associated with

---

17    Smedley and Smedley, 16–26.

how intelligent one is may seem confounding initially, but biology plays a role in how your brain is structured and functions.) However, the idea that there is a "racialized brain" is false.

Essentially, the idea that set categories of humans are racially different from each other is fiction. The categories were created by people who did not understand genetics. However, race continues to be used by the US Census, applied in scholarly and medical research, and socialized in America as scientific truth, even though it has been disproven in multiple ways by a wide range of scholars and scientists.

Racial categories in use today do not exist in nature. We create them and decide who belongs in which categories. We have the power to discontinue this falsehood for good.

CHAPTER 5

# How Race Upholds Power Dynamics

Each semester, one of my favorite things is seeing my students learn to use "the sociology words." Sociology has a language of its own. I love watching as they begin to understand and use words like "social class," "stratification," "inequality," "marginalization," etc.

Sociology introduces you to these words to frame how society is structured. I am always so proud when the students can use five or six words in a sentence at the end of the semester to say provocative things. Like, when they can say, "Your race is associated with your socioeconomic status," and truly understand what that means. These are my words based upon sociology words. Still, over time, they become the students' words as the students start to understand how they can be used to account for racism and racial inequality.

Every semester, the students begin understanding how social factors, like economics and race, shape their lives. When I see the illumination grow in their eyes, I know they see what

I see. They see that none of our experiences exists in isolation. Rather, our lives are a product, reflection, or defiance of our context. Among other insights, they can see how our understanding of race colors everything in our lives and how the myth of race upholds the dynamics of our society.

# The Racial Hierarchy Lives On

Race is all about economic and social power. It was created to measure who is allowed to participate in arenas such as the economy, politics, and other positions of power. To get economic and social power in America, you historically had to be White and male. This privilege was legally supported in the Constitution.

Historically *and* in modern times, your race predicts your **social location**, meaning how much status or power you have compared to others. Power comes in the form of educational attainment, job prestige, wealth, and other forms of cultural capital, which grant you status or the ability to act as you wish and get what you want. The racial order of the United States was historically White on top. The class system was further subdivided based on how light-skinned you were (hence the color gradient). Race remains a strongly predictive measure of which social class you belong to.

It may seem like the suppression of racial minorities is over, and that opportunity is now unlimited. But this trend continues globally into the present in some of the most foundational institutions in our society: housing, education, work, and wealth.

Entire books have been written on each of the following topics alone. For our purposes here, we are going to look at a broad overview of how institutional racism manifests across these arenas and how it perpetuates White privilege in concrete factors such as who gets approved more for mortgages, who gets hired more often, who receives more educational attainment, and who has more access to healthcare.

## How Race Upholds Inequality in Housing

Racism permeates numerous social institutions beyond the economy. Housing is perhaps one of the most fundamental, as one's access to housing—and the condition and location of that housing—shapes so many other factors in one's life.

Non-Whites experience statistically provable discrimination when applying for mortgages. Prejudicial attitudes attributed to mortgage lenders are attributed to stereotypes about someone's name, country of origin, skin color, language, and general culture, to name a few.

As an example, before the 1900s, there was no such thing as "Black areas" or geographical areas with an overwhelmingly Black population like there are today. Poor racial minorities and poor White immigrants lived in the same parts of the poorest parts of town.

However, with the rise of industrialization, racialized neighborhoods began developing. As people came to the Americas, they were drawn to people with similar ethnicities and lifestyles. As Asians arrived in the US, they were ranked between Whites and Blacks but were still relegated to living in areas with people who shared similar countries of origin. European descendants had a chance to work their way out of the slums, while non-European ethnic groups were stuck in the lower classes.

The Irish were relegated to areas with Irish populations, but as they blended into the White category over time, that distinction became less pronounced. The Irish could work their way out of poverty by gaining access to the political and legal arenas until they eventually became one with the ruling class. ("When did the Irish become White?" is always a favorite question.)

Immigration and migration patterns in the Americas go in multiple directions, but immigrants commonly flock to urban areas, especially following the Industrial Revolution. Cities have always been diverse in terms of ethnicity and socioeconomic status. However, the neighborhoods have historically been quite segregated by race, ethnicity, and socioeconomic status.

Racialized housing segregation is not a phenomenon of the past. Rural states have the highest rate of racialized residential segregation. As of 2022, Montana, Idaho, Wisconsin, and Maine had the highest rate of residential segregation, with over 75% of their residents being segregated along a Black-White axis.[18] But directly following rural states are the urban metropolises of New York, Illinois, and Pennsylvania, within which over 70% of their residents are residentially segregated by race.

Racism justified keeping racial minorities in poverty for most of American history. When you are stuck in poverty, you are less likely to attain homeownership, which accounts for why Whites are far more likely than Blacks to own a home, for example.

Furthermore, institutional policies blocked access to non-Whites from even hoping they could buy a house one day. It was often written into mortgages that Whites were not allowed to sell their home to someone who was not White. The ability to deny ownership to non-Whites was overturned by the Supreme Court

---

18    National Institute of Health, *Residential Segregation Table: Black/White Segregation* (National Institute on Minority Health, 2025), 1.

in 1948, but for generations, non-Whites were blocked from gaining a home for themselves. Therefore, people belonging to minority racial and ethnic groups living in the cities often were at the mercy of slumlords.

Another example of racialized housing policies involves urban development, often coinciding with the demolishing of minority neighborhoods. For example, when the interstate system was imposed, city planners went around the White neighborhoods in almost every US city. They put a road straight through the Black neighborhoods, destroying the value of the houses in those areas. Other institutional policies removed land once promised to Native Americans and gave it to White people. Other towns were "sundown towns," within which minorities could not be there after sundown without the risk of violence from Whites.

Theoretically, everyone should have access in modern times, but is that true? Do Blacks have the same fair shot as Whites to buy a house in a nice neighborhood with a good school?

For generations, countless White families have invested in their homes and passed that down to their children, along with other forms of assets and wealth. If Blacks had the same chance to get a house as Whites, inequality regarding the wealth gap between races would decrease and essentially be null and void.

Racism continues to be associated with mortgage practices. There is always a story in the news about how a Black, Hispanic, or Asian family was denied access to a house in place of an equally or under-qualified White family. Some of the saddest stories involve Black families having to strip all things that could be perceived as Black from their house and have a White couple stand in for them to get a good value on their home when selling it. Constantly, mortgage companies are being sued for appraising houses lower when they belonged to a Black family compared to a White family, or they outright deny them mortgages. For example, in 2024, the US Justice Department sued Rocket Mortgage and their appraisal company for undervaluing houses owned by Black individuals.[19]

This is such a limited look into the topic of housing discrimination, and it is already heartbreaking. The truth is that the arbitrary category of race still upholds housing inequality in the modern day nearly as much as it did decades ago.

## How Race Upholds Inequality in Schooling

Education is another area where racial inequality is prevalent. Blacks and Latinos are half as likely as Whites to complete a bachelor's degree, and Asians are more likely than all races to complete a degree.[20] Why is there a disparity between races and educational attainment?

We must delve into the association between culture and socioeconomic status to answer this question. Culture plays a significant role in the value systems internalized by those being socialized. One's culture influences decisions regarding whether to study and how important an education is. For example, Asian families tend to place higher emphasis on education than Whites, Blacks, and Hispanics, which translates into higher test scores and admittance to top-ranked colleges for Asians than

---

19    U.S. Department of Justice, *Justice Department Sues Rocket Mortgage, Appraisal Management Company and Appraiser for Race Discrimination in Mortgage Refinance Application,* (Department of Justice, 2024), 1.

20    Leah Shafer, *The Other Achievement Gap: The Lessons We Can Learn from Asian American Success,* (Harvard Graduate School of Education, 2017), 1.

other groups.[21] On the other hand, people who are more likely to be exposed to a culture of poverty, such as Blacks, Latinos, and non-Chinese or non-Japanese Asians, are less likely to graduate.

Regarding socioeconomic status, children growing up in well-to-do neighborhoods go to better schools, and in the US, well-to-do schools tend to be in resoundingly White neighborhoods. Growing up in the Chicago area, I remember that, as a kid, I always listened to my grandfather talk about the high-tax districts. It was common knowledge which towns were predominantly Black, Hispanic, Asian, White, or diverse. It was also common knowledge that the most desirable towns tended to be the White towns within which a few uber-successful minorities resided.

I didn't understand as a kid how taxes functioned as a mechanism of exclusion. It wasn't until I was way older that I began to see how towns and cities are structured according to race and socioeconomic status with my sociological imagination. As I grew up, I began to understand that how much money your parents had and what race you are dictated what neighborhood you grew up in and your chances for success. If you grow up in a great neighborhood with excellent schools, it is like being handed a set of opportunities that others may never receive.

Children in wealthier school districts benefit from higher funding, allowing schools to hire more experienced teachers and provide additional services. In affluent neighborhoods, schools and parent-teacher organizations (PTOs) have substantial financial resources. They can easily afford school supplies and build new facilities with money left over. I've seen this firsthand in my high-tax neighborhood in Columbus, Ohio. (*Full disclosure: I*

---

21   Shafer, 1.

*have kids! I want to live in the city while ensuring they get a quality education—please don't judge! But I digress.*)

High-tax neighborhoods are designed to exclude those who cannot afford the cost, limiting access to their well-funded school systems. While technically part of Columbus, my area has its own exclusive district where taxes are four times higher than in the rest of the city. As a result, local schools here operate with multi-million-dollar surpluses, and PTOs have hundreds of thousands of dollars in reserve. These funds provide opportunities that children in less affluent areas do not receive. Demographically, my neighborhood is about 86% White, 7% Asian, 6% mixed race, and 1% Black—a reflection of how economic barriers shape racial composition.

Therefore, if you stick an entire race in poverty, such as what happened with Asians, Blacks, and Latinos, educational attainment levels are going to take a hit. Asians did not historically get more college degrees than Whites. This is a recent trend, as Asians gained more access. However, the high educational trend does not hold up for *all* Asian groups—it is mainly for Chinese and Japanese Americans. The trend of low educational attainment continues for poor Whites, Blacks, Hispanics, and non-Chinese and non-Japanese Asians.

The historical exclusion of Black people from education is a stark example of how systemic inequality has shaped educational outcomes. Black people were excluded from education before and after Reconstruction. Whites knew that if Africans had an education, it would be more difficult to exploit them for their labor, and then Whites would have to pay for their education in the form of their taxes. The NAACP challenged separate but equal laws, and the Supreme Court ruled that integration was mandatory. However, this did not stop inequality in the education system between races. Black families are still trying to overcome racial domination that blocks their educational advancement.

When the schools were integrated in the 1950s, coinciding with the development of interstates, White flight occurred. White people with means did not want their children going to school with non-Whites, so they fled the cities and created havens of White neighborhoods in high-tax districts, where those who could not afford the taxes could not gain access to good schools and nice houses.

After the White flight, inner cities became havens of crime because the only people left in the town were those who were poor. Where there is poverty, there is desperation, and crime naturally increases. Furthermore, since the wealthy left the cities, the funding for the schools decreased. The neighborhoods slowly degraded, property values went down, and by the 1990s, you could buy a house in the city for next to nothing. Those who could not afford to leave were impoverished, and their property value sunk. Their neighborhoods went down, and their children were exposed to a culture of poverty and crime. During this time, you saw the rise of the crack pandemic and the highest rate of crime since the 1960s. The high-quality school systems remain in majority White neighborhoods in the suburbs. Although the inner cities have seen an increase in demand, the quality of the schools has not caught up.

Florida recently banned a book about Rosa Parks. In that book, Rosa Parks drives past the White school, which is beautiful. Then she arrives at the Black school, which is not the same quality. That was what it was like growing up Black in America pre-Civil Rights, but has it changed that much since? Black children continue to go to all-Black schools in primarily low-socioeconomic areas.[22]

The treatment of Native American children by Whites is another incredibly dark story in the history of the US education system. Native American children were stripped from their parents and forced to go to boarding schools run by Christians, where incredible atrocities occurred, abuses beyond imagination. We are still finding the unmarked graves of thousands of Native American children who were punished to death for not culturally assimilating to a White way of life. If Native American parents did not send their kids to these schools, they were imprisoned.

Ultimately, socioeconomic status begets life chances. Whites historically denied educational access to groups based on their skin color. Minority racial groups struggled for centuries to have a chance at a good education, to grow and develop enough to get a good job, to attain wealth and status, which begets autonomy, and to set their children up to do better. Children of racial minorities, just like children of poor Whites, are at risk for poor outcomes across the lifespan because they are more likely to experience the adverse effects of poverty, oppression, and violence. Education tends to be the number one way out of poverty, which is still denied to many along racial lines.

## How Race Upholds Inequality in Work and Income

At the time of this writing, the average Asian person in America makes $113,000 a year; the average White person makes $89,000 a year; the average Black person makes $56,000 a year; and the

---

22    Wang et al., "School Racial Segregation and the Health of Black Children," *Pediatrics* 149, no. 5 (May 2022): 1. https://doi.org/10.1542/peds.2021-055952.

average Hispanic person makes \$66,000 a year.[23] The disparity between racial groups has existed for generations. It is only in modern times that an Asian person makes more money than someone who is White. Blacks and Hispanics remain in poverty because of lower access to education and jobs, compounded by existing in a culture of poverty. Why is there a disparity in income between racial groups? How much of it is psychology, how much of it is growing up in a culture of poverty, and how much of it is due to prejudice and discrimination that blocks their access?

One answer is that social classes tend to be reproduced from generation to generation. In America, one can ascend the social class ladder, but the average person generally ends up exactly where their parents ended up.[24] Historically, being White was a requirement to rise up the social class ladder to attain wealth. Whites made more money, had better jobs, and had higher education levels, all contributing to socioeconomic status inequality. Recently, Japanese and Chinese Americans have achieved higher educational levels, job prestige, and wealth, on average, but this is only a recent trend, for historically, Asians did not have the opportunity to gain wealth. Most non-Japanese or Chinese Americans are still more likely to experience the effects of poverty.

Racialized poverty resulted from subjugating entire races of people into the lower classes. Racial minorities were not allowed managerial positions over Whites and were forced to take

23    Gloria Guzman, *Median Income of Non-Hispanic White Households Increased While Asian, Black and Hispanic Median Household Income Did Not Change*, (U.S. Census, 2024), 1.

24    Bhashkar Mazumder, "Intergenerational Mobility in the United States: What We Have Learned from the PSID, "*The Annals of the American Academy of Political and Social Science* 680, no. 1 (November 2018): 213–234. DOI: 10.1177/0002716218794129.

jobs in the lower-class workforce. Europeans took the land of Native Americans, usurped the land that was once Mexico, and interned the Japanese. They removed and denied citizenship to the Chinese and then later all Asians so that Whites could benefit from privilege. During the New Deal, Social Security, and then the GI Bill, minority races were restricted from benefiting. This occurred in all epochs of American society.

What happens when you stick an entire race in poverty? Even now that the doors have been opened more so than in the past for non-Whites, people who belong to minority racial groups are more at risk for being in poverty than Whites. Is it that they are simply lazy, and that is why they cannot climb the social class ladder, or is it an external attribution—that they live in a world that keeps people down? Getting out of poverty is not easy for any person, especially when they face institutional discrimination.

When a Black man looks out at the world and says, "If I go to college, can I get a good job?," what is reflected back? Does a Black man believe he can get a fair shot? Black males see the stigma in the world, and they internalize that. It affects an entire group's behavior and decisions. The awareness of racism keeps people down because they self-handicap, thinking they can never succeed because of the color of their skin. 13% of the United States citizens live below the poverty line, and most of those are White, due to the fact that there are more Whites than non-Whites in America. However, African Americans and Hispanics are two times more likely to be in poverty.

The causes of poverty are rooted in biology, psychology, and social context.

Biological factors like intelligence and genetics play a role. Psychological factors like cognition, emotions, motivation, and intelligence play a role. Social factors, such as economics, racism, quality of education, access to jobs, and region, play a role.

However, intelligence is deeply associated with social context. Becoming intelligent requires a social investment that challenges the brain's growth and development. Children who attend good schools tend to score higher on intelligence levels, not because of their race, but because of the quality of education and the fact that those kids eat daily.

The most important factor associated with intelligence is nutrition. Poor kids struggle with food insecurity and educational investment, which reduces their physical brain's ability to develop to its full potential. If you go to a good school and have proper nutrition, your brain will grow much healthier than those going to lesser-quality schools and experiencing food insecurity. This is unfair, but it is true.

It was not until after the Civil Rights Movement that non-Whites and females could gain capital for themselves. Up until then, only White males could compete to consolidate wealth. Since the Civil Rights era, White males have had to contend with racial minorities and females. However, institutional discrimination still plays a role in whether or not minority groups have a chance to raise their status. A Black and Hispanic middle class is growing, but it is still growing from stunted beginnings; the first time it ever had a chance to grow was after the mid-60s, when a Black man could finally get a managerial job or something more prestigious, like being a doctor or a lawyer.

Even with more significant opportunities today, getting a job is more complicated for women and non-Whites than White males. For example, institutional discrimination blocks promotion access and getting a call back for an interview. White-sounding names get the callback three times to one, and males get the promotions over females two times to one. In 2016, a study was done in which psychologists, one using a Black name and Black vernacular and one using a White name with a White vernacular, would leave phone messages requesting interviews.[25] They would then track the callbacks and find that White-sounding people with White-sounding names received more callbacks than people with Black-sounding names that sounded Black, even when their qualifications were the same.

Social relations are embedded in economics, and people's attitudes are associated with whether someone gets hired. Whether racial antagonism is conscious or unconscious, it exists, and people tend to hire people like themselves. Since White males in the US still dominate many industries, White males continue to hire White males more than they hire minority males and females. Power and privilege are maintained through social exclusion. Racial and gender minorities are forced to carve out space where they can find acceptance. Historically, females and racial minorities found room in service, caregiving, teaching, and medical service, except for being a doctor. It wasn't until the 1960s that doors opened for racial minorities, where they could carve out more space in arenas in which they were restricted, such as elite social positions.

Stereotypes also play a role in job attainment. For example, Blacks historically were stereotyped as being lazy and living off the welfare system to account for why they are in poverty. The truth is that Whites are way more likely to stay on welfare than

25    David Williams, "Stress and the Mental Health of Populations of Color: Advancing Our Understanding of Race-related Stressors," *Journal of Health and Social Behavior* 59, no. 4 (December 2018): 466–485. https://doi. org/10.1177/0022146518814251.

someone who is Black and Hispanic.[26] Blacks and Hispanics were stuck in poverty for generations with no way out, and now that there is a way out, it is still hard. Picking yourself up by the bootstraps is possible, but if it was that easy, why would there be poverty in the first place? The goal is to remove obstacles, such as racism, to enable more equitable access.

Is the economic system within which we live equitable? Does every American have a chance to rise up the social class ladder, or is that only for middle- and upper-class Americans? When Blacks were freed after slavery, they often had no choice but to return to the plantations to offer their labor. Just because they were free of the shackles of slavery did not mean they were free of the bondage of exploitation.

The same goes for today. Poverty in America is very real, and people who are in the lower classes do not have the capital to begin the process of working their way up the class system. When America's enslaved people were freed, they had little to nothing. Furthermore, they entered the social system that restricted their access and kept them down, whether it was through Jim Crow laws or simply denying them access to a college degree and a job.

Immigrants from all kinds of backgrounds in America have had similar experiences. When people came from Asia, they were exploited for their labor and restricted from accessing American institutions. Hispanics have been used for hundreds of years as an exploitable workforce. The same goes for the Irish, eastern Europeans, and most first-generation groups. Americans tried to enslave the Native Americans and used them as indentured servants, but they were worked to death.

---

26    Amanda ElBassiouny and Samantha Khan, "Impact of Race/Ethnicity, Veteran Status, and Place of Birth on Attitudes Towards Welfare Recipients: An Experimental Approach," *Psychological Reports* 124, no. 4 (August 2021): 1. DOI: 10.1177/0033294120953555.

Ultimately, racial lines do our society far more harm than good. They actively counteract the goal of creating a diverse and thriving workforce where all people are valued in the workforce and beyond.

# The Progress and Setbacks

Let us not forget that anti-racist movements have always existed. From the Underground Railroad to the marches on Selma, Montgomery, and Washington, D.C., people have fought against racial injustice. The Black Lives Matter movement continues this legacy, just as the Supreme Court rulings of the 1940s struck down Black voter exclusion and the 1960s progress overturned redlining policies that restricted Black homeownership. At the heart of these struggles was the Civil Rights Movement, culminating in the passage of the Civil Rights Act under President Lyndon Johnson. A Southern Democrat from Texas, Johnson made it his mission to fulfill John F. Kennedy's vision, using his influence to push the legislation through Congress.

With so much progress, why does racism persist? Because it remains an institution deeply embedded in American society. While organizations like the NAACP, SCLC, and SNCC were created to dismantle racist systems, racism itself has not disappeared. The marches from Selma to Montgomery and Washington, D.C., were historic, yet racial injustice still prevails. Marginalized communities must remain resilient in the face of hatred, constantly resisting the internalization of negative stereotypes perpetuated by racism in their daily lives. They are excluded because of their skin color, subjected to interpersonal discrimination, and forced to navigate a society built on institutionalized racism.

Race divides us. It convinces people they are different when they are not. It fuels inequality and negatively impacts socioeconomic status and health. Yet, like cigarettes, we can't seem to quit this harmful addiction.

We are caught in the constant struggle between progress and backlash. History is filled with movements aimed at restricting non-White communities. The Chinese Exclusion Act stripped citizenship from Chinese immigrants, followed by the broader Asian Exclusion Act. People have been interned, genocides have occurred, and ethnic cleansing continues in modern times. The Indian Termination Act forced Native Americans into cultural assimilation while White settlers stole their land and resources, pushing them into poverty. Native Americans fought back, most notably during the 1969 occupation of Alcatraz, which raised awareness of their struggles. Yet today, they remain among the most vulnerable populations in terms of health and economic security, a lasting consequence of cultural imperialism.

Cesar Chavez led the fight for Hispanic laborers, pushing back against the exploitative workforce upon which White capital was built. Arab Americans have long organized against discrimination, facing intensified prejudice after 9/11 and, more recently, in response to the Israel-Palestine conflict and Islamophobic rhetoric from right-wing politicians. Asian Americans have also resisted economic exploitation and racism, challenging the Eurocentric worldview and the distorted stereotypes imposed upon them.

Yet, with each step forward, White backlash rears its head. Slavery ended, but Jim Crow replaced it. Civil rights integrated schools, but White flight and rising property taxes ensured segregation by wealth. The KKK rose after the Civil War to crush Black progress, and today, White supremacists still march openly in our streets.

When will it be enough? Are we not ready to let go of something created generations ago by naive people who thought they understood genetics when they had just discovered a microscope? What would it take to get everyone to stop thinking of themselves as White, Black, or Asian, for example, and instead think of themselves as a person amongst people?

# CHAPTER 6

# Reimagining Identity Without Race

So, we now see that the racial categories we use today are not objective realities but shifting categories created by humans to establish and uphold power dynamics. But does that mean race is not *real*?

This reminds me of a story my good friend Neil told me. In college, he would come home after his sociology classes feeling energized by these profound realizations about race and his sense of identity.

When Neil got home, he wanted to talk about what he was learning. Neil's roommates, a group of engineering students, did not always receive Neil's intellectual enthusiasm very well. Neil would sit with them around the table with his elbows pressed into the wood and use overactive hand motions as he'd say, "Don't you see that races do not even exist?!"

Often, conversations like this would stir tensions. His roommates had been raised to see the world a certain way their entire lives. When Neil tried to challenge those ideas—to show them that the truth they'd believed for their whole lives may not be true after all—it caused them to dig in their heels even further. Our first instinct as humans is often to defend our existing paradigm and justify what we have always believed.

To reimagine our identity without race is a challenge, even for those who understand intellectually that race is a social construct that has done more harm than good.

I must clarify that to say race is not real, point blank, is not entirely true. When we socially construct something, we bring it into existence. We make it real. Just like if we create a new board game with a set of rules, those rules are fabricated, but if we are playing the game and collectively agree to recognize them, they are real and have real consequences in shaping our lives.

Race is real because our society operates by it; it is one of the most significant factors shaping our lived experience and how we relate to the world. We're driven to defend the idea not just because it's what we've always known but also because we have experienced the effects of these categories in our lives.

Even though my wife only learned she was "White" when she moved to America, she is still compelled to call herself White. She has a very different heritage than most other White people in America. At the same time, she recognizes that she is "White presenting" and benefits from White privilege by way of her appearance. (Unless she explicitly chooses to reveal that she is an immigrant, at which time others can decide what new category they want to place her in in their minds.) So even though the word White does not fully describe her, to call herself *not* White feels like a dismissal of the privileges she has been granted based on how others perceive her.

Her experience—and her conflicted feelings around her racial identifier—represent a core truth: Racial ideologies structure our lives. These lived experiences are real. At least in part, race determines our behavior, access, and social interactions. It's a factor that influences where we will grow up, how we will feel about ourselves in that context, what school we go to, who we will relate to, who we will alienate, what jobs we will have greater access to, and so many other factors that shape a life for better or worse. Race structures what is acceptable and what is not, who is to be judged, and who is not. Altogether, race is a significant part of our identity—whether we're conscious of it or take it for granted.

To discuss deconstructing race means to consider removing that piece of our identity. That is very hard to suggest. Being Black, for example, is an incredibly significant part of one's identity. It represents who they are and their connection with those who have struggled to take ownership of that identity in the face of oppression and marginalization. Our racial identity often fosters a sense of belonging to a larger group and others we can identify with.

If racial categories are arbitrary and even harmful, does disavowing them mean we also lose this sense of connection, identity, and solidarity? We do lose something in reforming our idea of race, but the answer is no. We don't have to lose these things we cherish. There is a key difference we must understand.

# The Differences Between Race and Ethnicity

To relinquish the concept of race is not to relinquish our identity, culture, or anything that comes with it. Why? Because none of those are inherently linked to our race to begin with. Rather, all those things we hold dear are products of our ethnicity.

I have had a transition in my mind wherein I no longer think of myself as a White person. I fully and passionately acknowledge that just because *I* choose to drop the category doesn't mean that others don't still see me as White. It doesn't mean I don't still benefit from the privilege of my status—both ascribed and achieved. It doesn't mean that my color and privilege have not shaped me. But it does mean that I don't need to hold Whiteness—a category strictly meant to give and take power—as a pillar of my identity. I still hold on to my ethnic identity as American, Irish, German, Welsh, and Cherokee. My ancestry is a part of me, but my race doesn't have to be because 1) my race is not rooted in scientific reality, and 2) I am opposed to the grounds the category exists upon.

Choosing to step away from Whiteness does not mean losing anything of real value. What matters to me—my family's traditions and cultural background—comes from my ethnicity, not my race.

We need to redefine and clarify our understanding of ethnicity as a society. Over time, race and ethnicity have been blurred into an ambiguous "race/ethnicity" category, but they are entirely separate constructs. They cannot be merged.

Like racial categories, ethnicity is a social construct. It is a shared identity built on core pillars like language, food, dress, customs, ancestry, worldview, and cultural background. This identity is primarily a matter of upbringing and what ways of life were socially imposed as "normal" as we developed our sense of self.

One's assigned racial category, or even one's biology, does not predict ethnicity. We see examples of this in children of immigrants and transnational adoptees who are culturally American, through and through, even though their ancestry might link them to a different part of the world. If they are not taught, nothing in their DNA will teach them the mother tongue or compel them to observe customary holidays.

Self-identification is key in terms of ethnicity. Because it is not genetically inherited, it is defined mainly by how much one identifies with and participates in the shared identity. As people age, they may shed cultural practices or threads that connect them to their ethnic identity. Conversely, someone who didn't grow up with a strong ethnic identity may seek stronger cultural ties with those with a common ancestry. Ultimately, one's ethnicity is defined by the group they identify with for a sense of belonging.

Scholars Mersha and Abebe explain, "Ethnicity is a complex multidimensional construct that reflects biological factors, geographical origins, historical influences, as well as shared customs, beliefs, and traditions among populations that may or may not have a common genetic origin."[27] Essentially, race is a system of categories based on differences that are thought to be biological. Ethnicity is a matter of culture and ways of life.

Though ethnicity is a social construct like race, it was created for a different purpose. Race was made arbitrarily by those in power to divide and conquer. On the other hand, ethnicity centers on the genuine commonalities that create belonging among a people group.

Of course, people can and do build prejudices on ethnic lines or believe their way of life is superior (ethnocentrism). I am not suggesting removing racial categories will solve this—we must tackle one "ism" at a time. However, I do believe a focus on

---

27    Mersha and Abebe, 1.

ethnicity is a far more helpful way of understanding the differences in our society.

# How Race and Ethnicity Became Adjoined

If race and ethnicity are so separate and developed in different ways, how did the constructs become so blended to where
they are (mistakenly) used almost interchangeably by so many?
Differences between socially defined races stem from cultural segregation—*not* genetics. This means that the only reason
there are separate race-based cultural groups in the US is because racial and ethnic groups were segregated for so long that
they evolved almost separately. Essentially, very different groups
of people were forced to share a common way of life in the US
until, eventually, they did.

As a result, race-based cultures evolved. For example, when
people from Africa first came or were forced to America, they
came from various countries, cultures, and languages. But because they were subjected to the same systems of slavery and
subjugation, the shared experience of Black people in America
became the new uniting cultural thread that bonded them and
gave them a "race-based" identity, which has become incredibly
tangible and influential in the years since. The same has happened with people in America from all over the globe who have
created a new subculture in America as a result of being lumped
together by an arbitrary racial category.

If there were no segregation, we would simply have American
culture. Morgan Freeman referred to this on *60 Minutes* when

he said he wanted to deconstruct Black History Month, which threw host Mike Wallace for a loop.

What Morgan Freeman meant when he said he wanted to deconstruct Black History Month was that Black history is American history. The point of constructing a Black History Month was to make it so voices rarely heard due to marginalization could finally have a voice.

However, why is Black history separated from American history when Black history is simply a part of American history? This is due to segregation. If no segregation existed, groups would not have their own segregated histories. American history would be American history, not subdivided into racial and ethnic groups.

However, even our history is segregated because racial minorities did not get a voice in its original telling. Instead, Europeans imposed the dominant culture of their making, engaged in cultural imperialism to destroy all non-European culture (such as renaming enslaved people with White names, stripping them of their religions, and imposing Christianity), and used force to ensure everyone followed the status quo established by the Europeans in power.

Hence, the origin of race-based cultures in America comes from segregation. Minorities were expected to live a White way of life but were also excluded from a White way of life. They were stripped of their culture, denied access to the dominant culture, and then had to build a culture anew in the Americas, borrowing from the old memories.

Therefore, race and ethnicity in America will be hard to disentangle. After all, we do not want to lose the sense of kinship that comes from people sharing in one another's experiences. However, we do want to dismantle the divisions that created

those subcultures in the first place, the racial categories that demarcate arbitrary differences between people.

# How Culture, Not Biology, Shapes Identity

At first glance, deconstructing race might seem like an attempt to
dismantle ethnic cultures—but that's not the case.

Ethnic identity holds deep significance in the United States.
Most Americans identify with a heritage beyond the US, referring to themselves as Irish, African, or Asian American. These
cultural ties run deep. To erase Black culture, for example, would
be to erase the history that shaped it—a history born out of slavery and segregation imposed by Europeans and their descendants. However, maintaining racial identity means upholding a
system of difference that perpetuates inequality based on country of origin and physical traits.

I am not calling for the dismantling of Black, Hispanic, or
any other cultural identity. I am calling for a clearer understanding of race and ethnicity. We must recognize that racial categories do not reflect biological differences. It's time to deconstruct
racial classifications—removing them from our ethnic identities
like a tumor that no longer serves us.

For example, we should acknowledge Black as an ethnicity—a culture-based on shared experiences, dialects, ways of
dress, heroes, music, and history—but not a race. To call Black
solely a race reduces it to a meaningless and inaccurate checkbox
institutionalized by White colonialists.

Similarly, we should also acknowledge that White, Hispanic,
and Asian are all real cultural groups, but they are not races. They

are not rooted in one's biology or even necessarily one's place of origin. Rather, these are **"panethnicities,"**—broad identities formed from exclusion, encompassing *multiple* cultural groups.

# Imagining Culture-Based Identity

When you ask yourself, "Who am I?" you look to the social categories stored in your mind to locate yourself. You may answer with, "I am a teacher" or "I am a musician." You may also answer with, "I am male, female, or intersex." You may answer with, "I am Black," or, "I am White." Race is a pillar of our identity because it is a pillar of culture.

How do we maintain our ethnic identity but drop our racial identity? Can we separate race from ethnicity? If we genuinely believe our racial systems only perpetuate injustice, how do we rise to the challenge of shedding them?

I don't know many people who think like I do when it comes to dropping my racial identity and creating a more equitable post-racial society. However, many notable people arrived at this idea before me. For example, one of the first people to suggest deconstructing race was political scientist Wilbur Rich. He stated that society should deconstruct racial categories in that they exist solely to maintain a system of White privilege. He still culturally identifies as Black but dismisses the identity as a racial category, proposing that our race-based society, our race-based identities, and racial categories should be deconstructed.[28]

Another inspiration for rethinking race-based identity came from queer theory. Queer theory challenges individuals

---

28  Wilbur Rich, *The Post-Racial Society is Here: Recognition, Critics, and the Nation State* (Routledge, 2015).

to consider whether we *must* categorize ourselves if we do not want to. It asks whether, instead of being a White, heterosexual male, for example, one can just be human. I like to question the categories because it presses me to ask myself: What would my life be like if my thoughts, experiences, and behaviors were not limited to conforming to a White, male, heterosexual cultural way of life?

Having no racial categories *would* remove an element of our identity, yes. But at the same time, it would remove the idea that we are in some way biologically different from other human beings when, in fact, we are all virtually the same. It would remove one fundamental basis of power imbalance and discrimination. It would allow us to focus on the cultural elements that unite us rather than the arbitrary and inaccurate differences that divide us and uphold our society's most insidious power structures.

The point of this book is to challenge us all to rethink everything we know about race. It is tough to deconstruct old knowledge, but the benefits of doing so are enormous. This deconstruction opens up the world to you. It begins to knock down years, decades, and centuries of walls and barriers, making way for a path of connection that goes on forever.

For years, I have tried to convince everyone I know that nobody belongs to a biological race. Some of my students and friends have taken on the challenge of disassociating themselves from their racial identity. Others just shake their heads at me, like my best friend Ronnie, who still insists I just call him Black (and get off my soapbox so we can resume our chess match in his garage). And that's alright; I get it. His Blackness means something very different to him than my Whiteness.

Still, I wonder if I got in Ronnie's head because I spent most of my master's degree in Ronnie's garage, exploring these ideas about race with him as I learned them. He would always be working on motorcycles, tearing them apart and, like the genius he is, putting them back together with ease from the chaos of parts strewn about the garage while I wrote papers about race and ranted about it to him for as long as he would listen. But it was also relevant for Ronnie. Being a Black man married to a White woman has social consequences—for them *and* for their kid, who must exist in this world, potentially caught between two categories. His son will be categorized by society as mixed, biracial, mulatto, or any other number of words because he is a child of an interracial couple. I often wonder if or how Ronnie will categorize his son and what opportunities or limitations those categories will impose on his life.

I, myself, want to live a life in which I don't restrict myself to being a White human. I want to go anywhere and feel like I fit in, no matter what the skin color blend in the room might be. I don't want to feel like an outsider if I'm the only light-skinned person around. I don't want someone else to feel like they're an outsider if they're the only dark-skinned person around. I spend my days trying to go beyond the category of White so that I can experience a more full life. I want to live my life on the baseline assumption that we all have infinitely more in common than we have differences. I want that baseline to drive curiosity, not scrutiny, toward those differences.

While it's certainly a challenge, and each person will have a unique approach to this challenge, I want the world to rethink whether they actually belong to the racial groups we use in modern times. I have used biological evidence to prove that humans are not different on a group level. I have made arguments supporting the idea that race was engendered in our society for European descendants to gain power over non-Europeans and remove competition from social and economic markets. All of this was done to debunk the idea that we are inherently different from each other.

Realizing you are not inherently different from someone else is life-changing. You can be part of groups you never once thought you had access to. Acknowledging that you are not different from the person beside you unravels your bias toward them. I am a firm believer that so long as we find each other different along racial lines, prejudice based upon racism will always exist in some form or another. But if we discontinue the use of race in society, we will set ourselves on the path to eliminating racism in modern society.

# CHAPTER 7

# Building a World Beyond Racial Categories

Everywhere we turn, we see calls to "end racism." It's painted in football end zones, printed on soccer jerseys, and echoed in corporate slogans. Yet, despite these symbolic gestures, racism persists. None of the proposed solutions have eradicated it.

As a society, we have dismantled scientific racism, proving that race is not biologically material and that distinct racial clusters do not exist. We have challenged and redefined the meanings attached to race. We have struck down discriminatory policies, passed Civil Rights legislation, and made institutional reforms. Yet racism refuses to die. Instead, it resurfaces—sometimes subtly, sometimes brazenly—because it is embedded in our society and within us. Whether implicitly or explicitly, we have all been conditioned by a system built on racial hierarchy. Until we confront this uncomfortable truth, racism will continue to adapt, finding new ways to thrive in a world that claims to reject it.

Why does racism continue despite positive changes in attitudes toward other groups? Racism continues because we have not deconstructed the root of the problem, which is the construct of race itself. So long as people think they are different, they will attach meanings to those differences. So long as race is an institution of our society, it will continue to perpetuate inequality between groups.

How would we reform society to reflect this truth? Leading research shows that the dismantling of race must occur on three levels: individual, interpersonal, and institutional. Individuals have their own beliefs, which they act on in relationships and which affect how we interact as a society. Each of these levels must be addressed to change the shape of society as we know it.

# Individual Reformation: Confronting Internalized Racism

It can be daunting to try to change society. However, a society is made up of individuals working together. So, to change our culture, we must first change the individuals and the society they wish to create.

On an individual level, change happens on the grounds of one's thoughts and beliefs. While our thoughts and beliefs are our own, we can't deny how the context in which we were raised trickles down to form how we think. If we are born into a world where racism still exists, we must acknowledge that it has seeped into our worldview, even in ways we are not conscious of.

To deconstruct racism on an individual level, we must start with an honest examination of how we have internalized the racism around us. We internalize racial prejudice in two primary forms.

The first belief we must acknowledge is how we have internalized racism toward ourselves. There is ample evidence that racism psychologically affects us and shapes our sense of identity. What others expect from us, especially in childhood or adolescence, influences what we expect from ourselves. As a parallel example, many young girls internalize sexism and subliminal messages about what studies or fields they should go into. Girls grow up thinking, "I'm a girl, so I'm bad at math." Studies show that girls who excel at math are more likely to study nursing, a predominantly female profession than continue to study math or science in male-dominated fields.[29] Similarly, if a young Black boy perceives that society stereotypes him as a criminal, he is more likely to lower his expectations of himself and take on deviant habits.

As the first step toward dismantling racism, I encourage you to reflect on how you may have internalized racial categories and biases toward yourself. How have you internalized stigma? How has it shaped your personality, decisions, where you choose to live, what neighborhoods you feel comfortable in, or what groups of people you avoid talking to?

To combat internalized racism, movements like the 1960s "Black is Beautiful" have emerged. This movement sought to reverse the racist messages about Eurocentric beauty standards and platform Black ethnicity, heritage, and natural beauty. We can build on movements like this and redefine our sense of self on our terms, not on racial lines.

In addition to internalized beliefs about ourselves, we

---

29    Alex Helman, Ashley Bear, and Rita Colwell (Eds.), "Promising Practices for Addressing the Underrepresentation of Women in Science, Engineering, and Medicine: Opening Doors," *National Academies of Sciences, Engineering, and Medicine,* (The National Academies Press, 2020). https://doi.org/10.17226/25585.

must examine the biases we have internalized about others. Resocializing oneself involves removing stereotypes, some of which have negative meanings and some of which are just heuristics.

If you have been told your whole life that you are different from someone because of your skin color, hair texture, or eye shape, questioning that knowledge can often be challenging because it requires thinking about yourself and others in a way you might never have thought of. Even with my knowledge and years of teaching about race and ethnicity, it is still hard to overcome all preconceived notions and deconstruct the meanings attached to skin color differences.

For example, with my light skin and my best friend's dark skin, we have been told our whole lives we are different. Indeed, we are different in our cultures, experiences, personalities, and talents, but we are not fundamentally different types of humans. To acknowledge this is the resocialization process. We have to stop thinking of ourselves as different from someone else based on the color of their skin, their ethnicity, or their geographic location—they are not biologically different. They may be different in their cultural identifications, but they are just as human as you.

Resocializing ourselves can involve simple steps. The first is to acknowledge our biases. What biases have you internalized about other racial groups? Which people are you most likely to introduce yourself to in a room full of strangers? Which neighborhoods would you avoid? Could you imagine yourself marrying someone of a different racial category or bringing them home to your family? Who are you uncomfortable around?

These insights are not meant to bring shame but to help us acknowledge that we are humans raised in a society of stigmas, and we must consciously filter out the bad.

# Interpersonal Reformation: Confronting Relational Racism

The individual level is all about our thoughts and beliefs. But once we act on those, they become interpersonal. On a relational level, internalized racism manifests through everything from micro-aggressions to hate crimes. The interpersonal level of change refers to how we let new beliefs shape our interactions with others.

Interpersonal change can be simpler than we think. It can be as simple as not using racial language when referring to someone. Instead of saying, "That Asian guy," say, "That guy with the yellow coat and the black shoes." We have to move beyond the easy and rethink everything. Go a step further and confront or correct a micro-aggression when you hear one from a family member, colleague, or loud politician. Even if it seems like no one agrees with you, your voice informs how the others around you interpret what is acceptable and what is not.

The most significant way interpersonal reformation happens is by exposing ourselves to new relationships. When we do this, we are effectively allowing ourselves to be resocialized. Try diversifying your friend groups. Studies show that the more exposure we have to people who are different from us, the less prejudiced thoughts we are likely to have.[30] Yes, we have different lived experiences, but fundamentally, we are all the same. Let that free you to find even more commonalities and learn from your genuine differences.

---

30    Mahzarin Banaji et al., "Systemic Racism: Individuals and Interactions, Institutions and Society," *Cognitive Research: Principles and Application* 6, no. 82 (December 2021). https://doi.org/10.1186/s41235-021-00349-3.

# Institutional Reformation: Confronting Racist Laws, Policies, and Attitudes

Institutional or structural reformation refers to changes in our systems, like government, housing, education, the economy, and the media. The more individuals change their beliefs, and the more those beliefs change their relationships, the more power we have to make changes in the institutions that structure our society.

The Civil Rights Movement made way for countless structural-level changes. After the Civil Rights reforms, discrimination based on race was no longer acceptable. Legalized segregation was invalidated. Interracial marriage was legalized. Affirmative action was engendered. But these movements did more than change laws. They shed light on the past and present struggles of Arab, Asian, Hispanic, and Native Americans. It made Americans aware of how Native culture was decimated, that slavery and the continued subjugation of Blacks was reprehensible, and it made us aware that White male privilege could be challenged.

Now, many of these hard-won gains are being rolled back. Efforts to ensure equal opportunities—regardless of race, gender, or disability—are being dismantled. Affirmative action is under attack. Women's reproductive rights are being stripped away. Anti-immigration policies defy economic logic and contradict the spirit of the Statue of Liberty. Politicians push false narratives about biological sex, ignoring the fact that 1–2% of people are born outside the male-female binary.

Meanwhile, Nazis march openly on American streets, protected by police. In *The Blues Brothers*, protesters drive them off
a bridge. Today, they stand *on* bridges in Cincinnati, flaunting
their hate as thousands pass by.

At the highest level, racism is a political tool. The US president openly exploits racial fears for votes. Trump's record speaks
for itself: banning Muslim immigrants, claiming Haitians "all
have AIDS," calling undocumented immigrants "animals,"
questioning Obama's citizenship, blaming crime on Black and
Hispanic communities, mocking Native Americans, and more.
He thrives on racism because his supporters share his views. His
words embolden those who harbor racial resentment but fear ex-
pressing it publicly. As influential figures amplify bigotry, social
attitudes shift, and racism is re-normalized.

As individuals, we can participate in institutional change
through many avenues. Of course, one avenue is voting to elect
people who uphold anti-racist attitudes at the federal, state, and
local levels. In our places of work, we can voice our support of
non-exclusionary policies. It has been shown that companies
with higher diversity tend to perform better overall, as higher
representation helps avoid "groupthink" and encourages more
perspectives toward a problem.

Sometimes, it is hard to act. You may feel scared, and you
may have a lot to lose. For example, Trump recently sent out an
executive order repealing DEI. I work in colleges. Shortly after
that order was sent out, all my colleagues and I received emails
from the presidents of their colleges letting them know that all
diversity, equity, and inclusion programs and committees were
disbanded immediately. The emails were not sensitive. There was
no mourning in their words. They were just a matter of fact.

It seemed like nobody regarded that ending these programs would negatively affect all of us fighting for a more just world. The chairperson of the diversity committee I was on put so much time and effort into making the world a better place, all without pay (it was a volunteer position), and the rug was pulled out from under them without concern.

At first, I was upset at the president for not standing up for something that strengthened and protected our community—and I still am. But I also acknowledge that the president had so much to lose, including millions of dollars in federal funding, which would bankrupt the college. So, what was the right thing to do in that situation? Do you prioritize the financing to protect business as usual, or do you sacrifice your standing and resources for what you know is right?

I acknowledge it's a difficult choice, but one thing is for sure: if no one pushes back, whoever lobbies the best will win. Politics is about vying for power to impose your will on others. I'm no politician, but I am lobbying as well. I am lobbying readers to replace outdated common knowledge and deconstruct racial categories on an individual, interpersonal, and institutional level. I am working to wield my influence to prompt us to find our voices and resist.

When you study social movements, violence is the number one method most often used to prompt social change. We have had countless episodes of violence over racial ideology—the Civil War, race riots, lynching, bombings, shootings, and stabbings. People have used violence to end racism. People have used violence to maintain a racist social system. Violence has not worked for either.

Let's try something more productive to end racism on an institutional level. Ending racism is, first, a war of words and thoughts. It requires people to shed outdated knowledge about race. It requires us to deconstruct racist ideology that supports White privilege. It requires us to stop thinking of ourselves as racially Black, White, Asian, Native American, Hispanic, Hawaiian, Pacific Islander, Alaska Native, or Some Other Race. It requires us to discontinue the use of race in our daily lives. We can and should hold on to our cultural identities, but let us let go of our racial identities, for they only perpetuate a system of inequality based upon false beliefs. Let us teach our children and ourselves that people are people.

Let the war of words and thoughts extend to our relationships and institutions. I hope to see equitable laws and policies reemerge—and a different system of categorizing the US population based on factors like socioeconomic status, geographic data, ethnicity, and language, which would paint a much more vivid picture of who lives here and what challenges they face.

# Future-Oriented Reformation: Teaching the Next Generation

As we approach the end of this book, you may feel the enormity of the task ahead. Implementing this scientific truth into our shared paradigms would require a comprehensive restructuring of how we live individually and collectively.

While I am optimistic about our ability to make progress here and now, I am also aware of the enormity of the task. For this reason, it will likely take generations to implement fully. I also understand many people will not be ready to drop their racial identity and deconstruct the use of racial categories in America.

But, as these ideas become more common knowledge—and they *are* becoming more common—we can teach the next generation the truth about race in the hope that they will construct a better society than the one we are born into. And I believe they can do it. After all, this society in which I exist now is far less racist than those in past times.

Let's empower the next generation to build on our shoulders. Children are not born racist, nor are they born understanding what differences mean. Children have to be told what the differences mean when it comes to races and ethnicities. Through socialization, we learn what each skin pigment means and which group it's associated with. Children do not know that someone who is Asian and someone who is Black are different, for example, until they are told they are different or they experience life differently and become aware of those discrepancies.

The hope of this book is that race will no longer be relevant one day as kids grow and make sense of their reality. To move toward this goal, I propose we guide the next generation in the following ways:

1. Teach the truth about the origin of race and racism in America. Don't be scared to talk about how Europeans and their descendants created racial categories and a racist social system that enslaved others so they could have privilege. That is the reality of our history. It is not to shame people but to teach what not to do as a society ever again. Have the uncomfortable conversation about Japanese Internment, how Native Americans ended up on reservations, and the Holocaust or people will forget, and history will repeat itself.

2. Teach that just because someone has a different skin color or is from a different country doesn't mean they are fundamentally different from you.

3. Teach that how someone looks should not determine their access to opportunities or the limit of how far their hard work can get them.

4. Teach that the government should not support racist policies and that we can use government to create a better world.

5. Teach that it's not okay to say things that exclude, diminish, or make undue assumptions of others.

Lastly, make an effort to keep your own words and attitudes in check. Children internalize everything we do, not just what we say. Model for them what you teach.

# Moving Forward Together

Deconstructing racial categories will expand equal opportunity for all by eliminating race-based barriers to opportunity. Without racial categories, one central mechanism of exclusion would disappear, allowing for a more meritocratic society where race no longer determines social mobility. Deconstructing racial categories won't eliminate all inequality—class, gender, and other disparities will persist—but it will dismantle race-based barriers that have historically denied opportunities based on skin color or ancestry.

If race were eliminated, we wouldn't see scenes like the one from my high school experience after moving from the North to the South—where all the Black kids gathered in front of the library while the White kids spread out elsewhere, rarely mixing. A false construct with no biological basis would no longer segregate society. Without racial categories, friendships and relationships would no longer carry a stigma. People could marry whomever they love without fear of prejudice.

Diversity is key to our very survival as humans, strengthening resilience against crises like pandemics. But even beyond the survival of our human race, diversity enriches society by fostering creativity, innovation, and empathy. Different perspectives lead to new ideas, stronger problem-solving, and deeper cultural understanding. A world without racial divisions would allow us to celebrate our unique heritages without using them to exclude or oppress. To thrive as a society, we must embrace diversity— not as a means of division but as a source of strength.

# The Beginnings of a World Without Race

**C**olonizing countries have recently come to grips with past racialized atrocities they have committed. For example, England's empire was built on subjugating minorities. They have since begun removing idols from their culture that historically were enslavers. As another example, the US Congress has apologized for past atrocities directed toward African Americans, Native Americans, and Hawaiian Americans. We have also begun removing the statues of racist Americans and taking other huge stances in the US, such as banning the confederate flag from NASCAR races, which at one point I never imagined possible. We are all dealing with the reckonings of our racist past and how it continues to affect the present and future.

With inklings of hope like this and perhaps foolish optimism, I genuinely believe we can unravel the grips of racism in our society. That is why I wrote this book: to play my role in ending it. To end racism would be to become a **post-racial society** in which everyone is valued equally based on their merits. I am not suggesting this means there will be no more racist individuals. I know enough to be sure that some will always harbor hatred and fear. Rather, I believe we can achieve a post-racial society in which race is not the underlying basis for who receives power and who doesn't. We can rework the infrastructure of our shared American culture to remove a vast majority of racist attitudes and structures so that children growing up in the future may only learn of its existence from our history books.

Join me in both imagining and actively working toward a world beyond race.

# Acknowledgments

For a book dedicated to unraveling racism in our society, it is only fitting that these acknowledgments honor those who have fought—and continue to fight—against it, whether by choice or because they have had no choice at all.

To those who came before me and those who stand in the fight today, I honor you. To the countless souls who have been murdered, beaten, raped, and brutalized by racism, I see you. To those who refuse to stay silent, even when the odds seem insurmountable, I stand with you. To those working to build a more just world, I thank you.

To this generation and those that follow, I charge you to embrace equity. One day, it will not be just the richest or the Whitest who rise—it will be the best and the brightest. And together, we will dismantle the falsehoods that divide us.

# Bibliography

Aiyetor, Adjoa A. "Social construction of race undergirds racism by providing undue advantages to White people, disadvantaging Black people and other people of color, and violating the human rights of all people of color." *University of Colorado Law Review*, 94, no. 7 (2023): 415–443.

Banaji, Mahzarin R., Fiske, Susan T. & Massey, Douglas S. "Systemic racism: individuals and interactions, institutions and society." *Cogn. Research* 6, no. 82 (December 2021). https://doi.org/10.1186/s41235-021-00349-3.

Bear, Ashley, Helman, Alex, Colwell, Rita (Eds.). "Promising Practices for Addressing the Underrepresentation of Women in Science, Engineering, and Medicine: Opening Doors," *National Academies of Sciences, Engineering, and Medicine*. (The National Academies Press, 2020). https://doi.org/10.17226/25585.

Bonilla-Silva, Eduardo. "The structure of racism in color-blind, "Post-Racial" America." *American Behavioral Scientist*, 59, no. 11 (May 2015): 1358–1376. https://doi.org/10.1177/0002764215586826.

Botha, Monique, & Frost, David M. "Extending the minority stress model to understand mental health problems experienced by the autistic population." *Society and Mental Health* 10, no. 1 (October 2018): 20–34. https://doi.org/10.1177/2156869318804297.

Bränström, Richard, & Pachankis, John E. "Country-level structural stigma, identity concealment, and day-to-day discrimination as determinants of transgender people's life satisfaction." *Social Psychiatry and Psychiatric Epidemiology: The International Journal for Research in Social and Genetic Epidemiology and Mental Health Services* 56, no. 9 (February 2021): 1537–1545. https://doi.org/10.1007/s00127-021-02036-6.

Coulson, Doug. "British Imperialism, the Indian Independence Movement, and the Racial Eligibility Provisions of the Naturalization Act: United States v. Thind Revisited." *Georgetown Journal of Law & Modern Critical Race Perspectives* 7 (May 2015): 1–42. https://papers.ssrn.com/sol3/papers.cfm?abstract_id=2610266.

Deng, Lian, & Xu, Shuhua. "Adaptation of human skin color in various populations." *Hereditas* 155, no. 1 (June 2017). https://doi.org/10.1186/s41065-017-0036-2.

Dentato, Michael P., Halkitis, Perry N., & Orwat, John. "Minority Stress Theory: An Examination of Factors Surrounding

Sexual Risk Behavior Among Gay & Bisexual Men Who Use Club Drugs." *Journal of Gay & Lesbian Social Services* 25, no. 4 (October 2013): 10. https://doi.org/10.1080/10538720.201 3.829395.

ElBassiouny, Amanda, & Khan, Sabith. "Impact of Race/ Ethnicity, Veteran Status, and Place of Birth on Attitudes Towards Welfare Recipients: An Experimental Approach." *Psychological Reports*, 124, no. 4 (August 2021): 1824-1844. doi:10.1177/0033294120953555.

Fabbre, Vanessa D., & Gaveras, Eleni. "The manifestation of multilevel stigma in the lived experiences of transgender and gender nonconforming older adults." *American Journal of Orthopsychiatry* 90, no. 3, (January 2020): 350–360. https://doi.org/10.1037/ort000.

Foeman, Anita K. "An intercultural project exploring the relationship among DNA Ancestry profiles, family narrative, and the social construction of race." *Journal of Negro Education* 81, no. 4 (2012): 307–318. https://doi.org/10.7709/jnegroeducation.81.4.0307.

Francis-Tan, Andrew, & Tannuri-Pianto, Maria. "Inside the Black box: affirmative action and the social construction of race in Brazil." *Ethnic & Racial Studies* 38, no. 15 (September 2015): 2771–2790. DOI: 10.1080/01419870.2015.1077602.

Fredrick, Emma G., Mann, Abbey K., Brooks, Byron D., & Hirsch, Jameson K. "Anticipated to Enacted: Structural Stigma Against Sexual and Gender Minorities Following the 2016 Presidential Election." *Sexuality Research and Social*

*Policy* 19, no. 1 (February 2022): 345. https://doi.org/10.1007/s13178-021-00547-0.

Goffman, E. *Stigma: Notes of the management of spoiled identity.* (Simon & Schuster Inc., 1963).

Guo, Guang, Fu, Yilan, Lee, Hedwig, Cai, Tianji, Mullan Harris, Kathleen, & Li, Yi. "Genetic bio-ancestry and social construction of racial classification in social surveys in the contemporary United States." *Demography (Springer Nature)* 51, no. 1 (February 2014): 141–172. https://doi.org/10.1007/s13524-013-0242-0.

Guo, Guang, Fu, Yilan, Lee, Hedwig, Cai, Tianji, Mullan Harris, Kathleen, & Li, Yi. "Recognizing a Small Amount of Superficial Genetic Differences Across African, European and Asian Americans Helps Understand Social Construction of Race." *Demography (Springer Nature)* 51, no. 6 (November 2014): 2337–2342. https://doi.org/10.1007/s13524-014-0349-y.

Shafer, Leah. "The Achievement Gap: The Lessons We Can Learn from Asian Educational Success." Harvard University Graduate School of Education, 2017. https://www.gse.harvard.edu/ideas/usable-knowledge/17/04/other-achievement-gap

Hatzenbuehler, Mark L. "Advancing Research on Structural Stigma and Sexual Orientation Disparities in Mental Health Among Youth." *Journal of Clinical Child and Adolescent Psychology* 46, no. 3 (December 2017): 463–475. https://doi.org/10.1080/15374416.2016.1247360.

HDPulse. "An Ecosystem of Minority Health and Health Disparities Resources." National Institute on Minority Health and Health Disparities, 2025. https://hdpulse. nimhd.nih.gov/data-portal/physical/table?age=001&age_ options=ageall_1&demo=01005&demo_options=res_ seg_2&physicaltopic=100&physicaltopic_options= physical_2&race=00&race_options=raceall_1&sex=0&sex_ options=sexboth_1&statefips=00&statefips_options=area_ states.

Ifekwunigwe, Jayne O., Wagner, Jennifer K., Yu, Joon-Ho, Harrell, Tanya M., Bamshad, Michael J., & Royal, Charmaine D. "A qualitative analysis of how anthropologists interpret the race construct." *American Anthropologist* 119, no. 3 (August 2017): 422. https://doi.org/10.1111/aman.12890.

Lazaridou, Felicia, & Fernando, Suman. "Deconstructing institutional racism and the social construction of Whiteness: A strategy for professional competence training in culture and migration mental health." *Transcultural psychiatry* 59, no. 2 (April 2022): 175–187. https://doi. org/10.1177/13634615221087101.

Lund, Emily M. "Examining the potential applicability of the minority stress model for explaining suicidality in individuals with disabilities." *Rehabilitation Psychology* 66, no. 2 (2021): 183–191. https://doi.org/10.1037/rep0000378.

Major, Brenda, & O'Brien, Laurie T. "The social psychology of stigma." *Annual Review of Psychology* 56 (February 2005): 393–421. https://doi.org/10.1146/annurev.psych.56.091103. 070137.

Mazumder Bhashkar. "Intergenerational Mobility in the United States: What We Have Learned from the PSID." *The Annals of the American Academy of Political and Social Science* 680, no. 1 (November 2018): 213–234. https://doi.org/10.1177/0002716218794129

Mersha, Tesfaye B., & Abebe, Tilahun. "Self-reported race/ethnicity in the age of genomic research: its potential impact on understanding health disparities." *Human Genomics* 9, no. 1_ (January 2015). https://doi.org/10.1186/s40246-014-0023-x.

Meyer, Ilan H., Schwartz, Sharon, & Frost, David M. "Social patterning of stress and coping: Does disadvantaged social statuses confer more stress and fewer coping resources?" *Social Science & Medicine* 67, no. 3 (2008): 368–379. https://doi.org/10.1016/j.socscimed.2008.03.012.

Murray, Charles. *Human Diversity: The Biology of Gender, Race, and Class* (New York City: Twelve, 2020).

Perez-Rodriguez, Javier, de la Fuente, Alejandro. "Now Is the Time for a Postracial Medicine: Biomedical Research, the National Institutes of Health, and the Perpetuation of Scientific Racism." *American Journal of Bioethics* 17, no. 9 (September 2017): 36–47. DOI: 10.1080/15265161.2017.1353165.

Parker, Kim, Menasce Horowitz, Juliana, Morin, Rich, Hugo Lopez, Mark. "Multiracial in America: Proud, Diverse, and Growing in Numbers." Pew Research Center. (June 2015). https://www.pewresearch.org/social-trends/2015/06/11/multiracial-in-america/.

Rich, Wilbur C. *The Post-Racial Society is Here: Recognition, Critics, and the Nation State*. (Routledge, 2015).

Rocha, Zarine L., & Yeoh, Brenda S. A. "Orang Cina Bukan Cina: being Peranakan, (not) being Chinese and the social construction of race in Singapore." *Identities* 30, no. 4 (November 2022): 1–20. https://doi.org/10.1080/107028 9x.2022.2145775.

Rogers, Leoandra O., Scott, Marc A., & Niobe, Way. "Racial and gender identity among Black males: An intersectionality perspective." *Child Development* 86, no. 2 (November 2014): 407-424. https://doi.org/10.1111/cdev.12303.

Sotka, Erik E. "Clines." *Encycolpedia of Ecology 2ⁿᵈ Ed* (2008): 26-31. https://doi.org/10.1016/B978-0-444-63768-0.00469-8

Smedley, Audrey. ""Race" and the construction of human identity." *American Anthropologist* 100, no. 3 (September 1998): 690–702. https://doi.org/10.1525/aa.1998.100.3.690.

Smedley, Audrey, Smedley, Brian D. "Race as biology is fiction, racism as a social problem is real: Anthropological and historical perspectives on the social construction of race." *American Psychologist* 60, no. 1 (2005): 16–26. https://doi. org/10.1037/0003-066X.60.1.16.

US Census Bureau. "Population Estimates Program (2023). https:// www.census.gov/quickfacts/fact/note/US/RHI625221#:~: text=OMB%20requires%20five%20minimum%20 categories,report%20more%20than%20one%20race

Wang, Guangyi, et al. "School Racial Segregation and the Health of Black Children." *Pediatrics* 149, no. 5 (April 2022). https://doi.org/10.1542/peds.2021-055952.

Williams David R. "Stress and the Mental Health of Populations of Color: Advancing Our Understanding of Race-related Stressors." *Journal of Health and Social Behavior* 59, no. 4 (November 2018): 466–485. https://doi.org/10.1177/0022146518814251.

Zuberi, Tukufu, Patterson, Evelyn J., & Stewart, Quincy T. "Race, methodology, and social construction in the genomic era." *Annals of the American Academy of Political and Social Science* 661, no. 1 (September 2015): 109–127. https://doi.org/10.1177/0002716215589718.

# About the Authors

## Dr. Kevin Coghlan

Dr. Kevin Coghlan grew up in Chicago, IL; Nashville, TN; and Columbus, OH. He holds a PhD in Psychology with a specialization in Gender Diversity from National University and a Master's in Sociology from Middle Tennessee State University.

Dr. Coghlan is a professor of psychology and sociology. His teaching focuses on social stratification, particularly concerning race and ethnicity, social class, biological sex and gender, and sexuality.

He lives in Upper Arlington, OH, with his wife, Ina, and their two children, Beckett and Harlow. In his free time, he enjoys coffee and playing live music.

## Maureen Pelegrin

Maureen Pelegrin has worked as an Intervention Specialist in Cleveland, Ohio, and its surrounding suburbs for over fifteen years. Her experience spans diverse educational settings, from low-income urban schools to affluent districts, giving her firsthand insight into the systemic inequalities that shape students' educational opportunities. Passionate about advocating for equity in education, Maureen is committed to supporting marginalized students and challenging the structures that reinforce racial and socioeconomic disparities.

In her spare time, she enjoys de-stressing with family and friends, swimming, and practicing yoga.

www.ingramcontent.com/pod-product-compliance
Lightning Source LLC
Chambersburg PA
CBHW072235290326
41934CB00008BA/1303